REIGNITING HOPE
Spark The Fire To Grow Hope In Your Life.

By Tricia Andreassen

Co-Authored by:
Anna Brehm Anderson
Desiree Anderson
Peg Arnold
Kate Bancroft
Wendell Betts
Laura Campbell
Jacquie Fazekas
Marilee Harrington
Jennifer Johnson
Krista Morrissey
Eden Adaobi Onwuka
Edward Reed
Janea Trapp
Carlos Vargas

Creative Life
Publishing & Learning
INSTITUTE

Creative Life Publishing & Learning Institute
www.CLPLI.com
Info@CLPLI.com

Book Versions
Paperback ISBN: 978-1-946265-14-2
eBook ISBN: 978-1-946265-15-9
Amazon ISBN: 978-1-946265-16-6

Cover Design By Dara Rogers

CONTENTS

DEDICATION

This book is dedicated to the Founder of *Rising Hope Farms* Gail Wartner, the volunteers and to the loving horses who openly give their love to create a rising hope in the lives of mentally, physically and emotionally abused children.

This farm has been a blessing in my life. I am given a great dose of therapy every time I get my *"snuggles"* from my favorite boy Prophet and the other the horses.

Because of them, my hope rises and my lyrics in this book is also a tribute to them. One early morning as I sat in the barn with them I felt God's presence. In that moment I began to sing, *"Because of you, my hope rises."*

To learn more about *Rising Hope Farms*, their ministry and to donate go to www.RisingHopeFarms.com.

This book is also dedicated to my co-authors who pour into me a fresh dose of hope right when it is needed. I love you all and I am blessed to have you in my life.

I also dedicate this book to my husband Kurt and my son Jordan who are the special men in my life. I love you more than words. Thank you to my Heavenly Father who is my daily Hope. This work I do is my work for Him.

- Tricia Andreassen

FOREWORD

"Rock bottom is laced with razor blades" was my description of that dark place where life seemed absolutely hopeless. In that moment, the worst of my past was completely defining my future. I'd been a victim of different types of abuse for so long that flirting with despair was normal. That time was just much worse than normal.

No hope.

Hopelessness. Depression. Deadly darkness. Suicide?

Fortunately, my life didn't end there. Ten years later, I was still alive and kicking. Because of HOPE. Hope that something ahead was worth living for. Hope was the speck of light coming through into the prison of abuse and pain that had trapped me for most of my life.

Not everyone has horrific stories of abuse. I'm praying you don't. But hope is still the emotion that makes waking up every morning worth it. Hope is what motivates you to face each challenge in life. Hope lights your way when darkness starts creeping into view. Hope gives buoyancy to life when the cares of this world weigh you down.

What role has hope played in your life? Are you needing more hope?

I'm always looking for ways to add and multiply hope in my life and the lives of others. Now that my life has been miraculously restored, my consistent message to fellow abuse victims is *"You're not alone. There is hope."* I encourage each Ex-Victim to share his/her journey because our stories of finding hope can spark the fire of hope in others.

Tricia Andreassen, Ms. Unstoppable, is passionate about igniting hope in your heart. Tricia has lived through countless times when hope gave her the spark to keep moving forward. To keep living. To keep overcoming the obstacles in her life.

In *Reigniting Hope: Spark The Fire To Grow Hope In Your Life,* Tricia and her fellow contributors share how they have walked the paths where hope was lost, rare or a struggle to find and hold onto. They've been where you are. They have learned many secrets to finding more hope. Their stories, lessons and questions will open your mind to the possibilities hope creates and the life it fuels.

HOPE.

No matter what your story is, you can benefit from more. A lot more. Copious amounts. There is no such thing as too much. Ever.

HOPE.

If you've been struggling with finding hope for your future, sit back. Relax.

Read hope.

Breathe hope.

Dream hope.

Share hope.

Join Tricia and her hope-filled team on this beautiful journey to a future alive with hope.

- Paula Mosher Wallace
Founder and President of *Bloom In The Dark, Inc.*
Producer and Co-host of international television show, *Bloom Today*
Author of *Bloom in the Dark: True Stories of Hope and Redemption*
Franklin, TN

THE LIGHT COMES AT THE DARKEST MOMENTS

By Tricia Andreassen

THE LIGHT COMES AT THE DARKEST MOMENTS

It's the morning of my birthday, Dec 21, 2017 and I have no idea how to put words together. It has been so long since I felt my fingers hit the keyboard to the level of just getting lost inside of the written word. All I know is that I am having feelings on this birthday that one never hopes to experience.

There are cheerleaders who will say, *"Come on Tricia! Start the day with a smile on your face and life will get better! Walk around the house praising God and don't let anything get you down."*

So perhaps I am writing this to someone who feels like, *"Yeah, right... that is easier said than done."* I've filtered through so much advice, delivered in a multitude of ways as I sit in the quiet remembering all the comments. NUMB. Yes Numb. When reading this chapter, you may question how the main author of this book could be so candid about describing how miserable life can be! You may be thinking, *"I bought a book about Hope! I thought this lady and the co-authors sharing their stories planned to deliver a miracle solution to lift me out of all this pain."*

Interesting isn't it, how life works? One minute everything is going along great and the next it feels as if the floor is caving in around you. In moments of darkness we search that deep dark without a flashlight, a lantern or even a candle to just see the hand in front of us, much less the path ahead.

We have to keep walking. There's no other choice, but let's get real. It's dark out there and downright scary. If you have ever had a moment of complete darkness that left you uncertain of your surroundings you know how it is. With outstretched hands, you feel along the edges of furniture in your home, searching for glasses, clothing or anything that could be useful in the hunt for light. The scenario is ironic because the darkness is so profound, glasses wouldn't help anyway. The process is so debilitating you don't know which clothes to reach for, and frankly you just don't care at the moment. You just need something...anything to help you find the light switch.

I know someone who picks up this book will know exactly what I am talking about. You are just about out of hope, and may not even tell anyone. Why not tell? Because you are the type of person that appears to have it all together. Shoot, you go to church! You have your own marinated 'war room'! If you told someone that your own flame of hope was dim, what would be said behind your back? *"Mmm, here she talks a good game but when the chips are down she doesn't have what it takes. She can't even master it herself!"* The part of the mind that nourishes insecurities continues to pluck away at any warmth, any identity or any assurance you may still possess. Your mind conjures up entire conversations. *"Here she is saying she's got it all together and just look at her now. She doesn't even know how to do it herself much less write a book on it! Who does she think she is?!"*

Yes...that ever-churning mind of ours. It can take over our whole existence if we let it. Maybe that is why I knew my name was *"Unstoppable."* It's a word that I gave to myself long ago, a walking affirmation, *"Tricia, you got this. Come on, girl. You're unstoppable!"* It was part of the pep talk I recited to myself while driving in the car playing the game of *"10 things I am grateful for right now."* Yes, that good Ole' Ms. Unstoppable would take over to get the scared Tricia through those darkest days.

Have you ever had a day where you just don't know how much more can be thrown at you?

Man, I do.

The worst attacks come to me mostly through a specific way. I say this because the other day I was listening to the wonderful T.D. Jakes on his YouTube channel and he was talking about this. He explained that we are attacked in the area of our greatest strength so the devil can take us down fast. It reminds me of a boxing fight. When I was little my dad loved to watch the boxing matches on television. I would sit with him and watch as a way to bond. Honestly, I didn't like watching men beat up on each other. I didn't like how the winner took the other person down, much less throw the worst punch when the other fighter was wobbling on his feet. I cringed at the punch that took the losing boxer down and ensured he STAYED DOWN FOR THE COUNT. Maybe that was my first clue of how I was engineered. You see, my greatest strength is in connection through communication and relationship building. I have always been the one in my heart that steadies someone who is wobbling. I come in and try to hold them up, coach them through the ordeal and even stand in front of them as a warrior to protect them against the raging battle. But, as I have said, our strengths can be turned into a weapon against us if we aren't careful.

So, the devil turns it straight around on me and takes me out just like one of those fighters in the ring. Sometimes it's a glove for a glove eating away at my stamina, bit by bit, and other times it's a blow that takes me down. BAMM! It's in those moments where I feel like my whole body hurts and the lights have been turned off. I can't see anything, but can I feel every single ache. I feel pain in places that I would do anything not to feel. Those debilitating words, *"See, you can't do anything right."* Or, *"I told you that you were going to be a failure even (so and so) who is supposed to always love and support you thinks you are worthless. You know all of this is all your fault."*

How does one find hope when every which way you look it seems dark?

Many things have helped me greatly along with journaling, reading my Bible, art, singing, photography and more. One is creative visualization techniques and I would like to take you through that as I have done myself. In fact, I will do it with you right now as I write this to you.

If you can, trust me and do this right now.

Imagine yourself at a crossroads. You can turn 360 degrees and you can see five different paths. It is as if though you are in the middle of the spokes of an old wagon wheel. There are so many roads to choose from and walk down but in your observation, you notice a flicker of light along a path catching your eye. Why is it that this path has a light? You are confused. Tired. Lonely. Broken. You decide to investigate this flickering light. It's a way off in the distance but you know it's a sign of some kind to get you there, to show you something.

In faith, you begin to walk the chosen path to investigate the little flicker of light. As you draw closer you notice it isn't just one light. It is in fact a series of candles aligning each side of the road leading you to this large warm fire at the end of the destination. As your walk continues you begin to see signs interspersed among those candles. The signs say,

"It's ok. I believe in you."

"God is here, just talk to Him"

"You are never, ever alone."

"No wrong doing can take the place of the good works God has in store for you."

"You are loved."

"Never turn back and give up."

As the walk continues, you begin to realize the signs are hand written. The individual candles have been lit by specific people to help you. At the end of the path is the most beautiful fire pit one could ever envision. The warmth is so enveloping you are amazed at how comforted you feel. You no longer feel that you are alone and in a dark place. A big chair is located next to the fire just waiting for you to sit and take in all the love that is coming around you.

Scriptures are carved into the heavy wood of the chair. They are there for you to read before you sit down as well as to meditate on. You sit there in the presence of this experience. In addition, scriptures have been strategically placed on the arm rests so as you lift your arm you can read more, feeling reassured.

Those scriptures say...

"We are foreigners and strangers in your sight, as were all our ancestors. Our days on earth are like a shadow, without hope."
1 Chronicles 29:15

"For in this hope we were saved. But hope that is seen is no hope at all. Who hopes for what they already have?"
Romans 8:24

"But as for you, be strong and do not give up, for your work will be rewarded."
2 Chronicles 15:7

"You are the light of the world. A town built on a hill cannot be hidden."
Matthew 5:14

"In the same way, let your light shine before others, that they may see your good deeds and glorify your Father in heaven."
Matthew 5:16

"...And surely, I am with you always, to the very end of the age."
Mathew 28:20

"The following night the Lord stood near Paul and said, 'Take courage! As you have testified about me in Jerusalem, so you must also testify in Rome.'"
Acts 23:11

A kindle is sparked.

You aren't certain how it has happened or what you just experienced but you know a feeling has been rekindled in you. A warm stirring in your belly has swelled up in your heart. You are reminded that you don't walk alone. There are many paths to choose from, and you can choose one that has some light (even if it seems dim at first.) The longer you sit there the greater the warmth that surrounds you. The fire seems to burn a little brighter minute by minute, and out of the shadows come those people who lit a candle to help show the way. They were called to light those candles because at some point in their lives they walked the same path as you. And, truth be known in reality they still have moments of walking that path and feeling lost and alone.

The people who are meeting you at the fire pit have gathered together to pour into you and to remind you that God is here and so is hope. Each person gathered around you is one of the authors here in this book.

My hope is that you can know that *Hope* is always waiting for you. Hope is always available to you. Hope is inside you. It may feel like the ember of the flame is just about burnt out but trust me, give yourself to this process and ask God to light the way to the teachings you need to hear, right now. He will ignite the fire within your soul that brings hope back alive.

STRATEGIES FOR IGNITING YOUR FIRE OF HOPE

1. What are some challenges that you feel you are dealing with right now?

_____

_____

_____

_____

2. On a scale of 1-10 where is your hope right now? Why?

_____

_____

_____

_____

3. Be completely open with yourself and write in this book. Writing has helped my heart and strengthened my resolve immensely. What form of healing do you want in your life right now? How important is it to you? Are you willing to dedicate yourself to the process as if your life depended on it? Let your thoughts flow now.

_____

_____

_____

_____

_____

_____

_____

4. Look forward 6 or even 12 months from today. What do you want for your life? Imagine it has happened and it is a year later. Write as if a year has passed since you read this book and things have transformed to bring great healing and transformation. Start the writing with this prompt.

It's been a year since I bought this book and I am amazed at the wonderful things that have happened to me since that day I opened those pages. I thank you God for giving me...

Continue with prompts such as **I never knew that my hope would grow to a level that would give me...**

Allow the Holy Spirit to work through you as you read these stories and hear the voices of these wonderful people coming around you to support you and to love you. Because of you, I have hope too. You see, when I share my heart with you I feel like I have a friend who is there for me. Just knowing you are reading this book and willing to take these steps gives me the strength to continue on as well.

As Romans 6:5 says *"For if we have been united with him in a death like his, we will certainly also be united with him in a resurrection like his."*

_____

_____

_____

_____

_____

_____

_____

_____

_____

_____

_____

_____

_____

_____

ABOUT TRICIA ANDREASSEN

Tricia Andreassen has a fire within her heart that started when she was a youth camp counselor. *"My mission is to bring teachings and life strategies to help break through struggles and obstacles that may arise. We all have a purpose and calling for our lives and I want as many people as possible to discover what their heart calls them to do."*

Tricia's unique combination of walking this path allows her to help others fulfill their life dreams. As an entrepreneur herself, Tricia bought her first real estate investment property at age 19. Her passion for growing leaders led her to be a National Speaker and Trainer for Realtor.com®, the official internet site of the National Association of REALTORS® (NAR). After seeing a deeper need to help real estate agents and teams develop their business plans, brands, websites and marketing messages, she started Pro Step Marketing from the bonus room of her house with her toddler son literally on her hip. She grew Pro Step Marketing into a leading marketing, web development, coaching and strategic planning company in the real estate niche; creating strategies and plans for more than 50% of the top REALTORS® listed in production for the Wall Street Journal. After almost 15 years as CEO, she sold her company.

In 2007 another life shift happened within Tricia's soul, and she began writing songs. Her heart yearned to help others through life challenges due to her own discoveries within herself. The unlocking of this spiritual and creative heartbeat in her opened her dreams of recording her own CD, singing at a national conference with over 7,000 in attendance and writing her first business book which has led to writing for magazines, news organizations, personal development and fiction. As her journey progresses, she evangelizes the message of persistence, resilience, faith and other life strategies with the spiritual gifts of soul healing work. Her passion is to deliver God's word and inspiration through writing books, speaking, teaching, singing and songwriting that speak resilience and life transformation.

Over the last 25+ years she has helped thousands of people in their lives and business. One of her companies, Creative Life Publishing and Learning Institute supports this mission of helping writers become authors as well as fostering teaching and training programs in faith, leadership, youth, parenting, business building, marketing and spiritual growth. All the authors that are published are personally interviewed and selected by Tricia with the highest integrity. Tricia's business and marketing book hit number one in less than five hours and was continually on the best-seller list for 59 weeks. She is also a Certified Speaker and Coach for the John Maxwell Organization to teach leadership, personal growth and youth development programs as well as a Certified Executive Coach through ACTP credentials for the International Coaching Federation, which enlists uniquely creative strategies to work with organizations, schools, ministry groups and leaders from all walks of life. In addition to this work she is an active speaker, songwriter and singer.

To inquire about Tricia speaking at your next event email Warrior@MsUnstoppable.com or visit www.MsUnstoppable.com. If you have a story or message inside of you that could bring positive changes to others or a desire to be an author or speaker please reach out to Tricia today for a confidential conversation. To book Tricia as a speaker for your next event or to lead a retreat, a call with Tricia is essential as the first step to assure that she helps you achieve the outcome for success. Not all topics are listed on her website as some are designed custom for her clients and the specific topic of the event. She is also available for sermons and worship singing at your church or faith based conference.

Contact Tricia:

- Website: www.MsUnstoppable.com
- LinkedIn: www.LinkedIn.com/in/TriciaAndreassen
- Facebook: www.Facebook.com/UnstoppableWarrior
- YouTube: www.UnstoppableWarriorWithin.net
- Twitter: www.Twitter.com/TriciaSings
- Instagram: www.Instagram.com/MsUnstoppableWarrior
- Radio Show: www.UnlockYourInnerWarrior.com

HEAVY BURDEN

By Tricia Andreassen

HEAVY BURDEN

Dear Lord, it is early morning here at 4:40am. Lord, I need your help so much. I do not want to go into the New Year with this sadness in my heart, which feels as if though a heavy weight has been attached to it. I know my heart has been broken but God I know you are the only one that can heal a broken heart fully. You are the master healer and I must place my hope and trust in you that you are organizing all for my good.

I pray so specifically today that you help me have an unwavering focus for your work. I pray that you guide my steps. I pray that you help me write what I am to write this morning. Please help me not get distracted and to stay focused on the work you have called me to do. I need a deep healing, Lord, within me. I feel like I have been strong for so long that the places people don't see are crumbling. God, only you can give me the repair. I realize that I have looked to other people to repair my heart and I can't any longer. I must give it to you.

I visualize a scene of walking down the isle of an old church, carrying a basket in my hands. The basket holds the troubles, the past, the people I am praying for, the hurt of my heart, the pain that I am carrying for others and the self-blame. The basket is extremely heavy and large, so much so that as I walk down the aisle toward the alter I can't even see it but I know it is there. I keep walking forward. I refuse to give up because I know that once I get there the basket will be placed at your feet. It will be passed to you. I will no longer have to feel so tired from carrying this basket for such a long way and a long time.

Step-by-step I hold myself steady while struggling with this very heavy basket. As I move closer to the altar the weight of it in my arms is more pronounced, making it difficult to walk. My hope is that I will be successful. My faith and trust knows that once I lay it at the altar I will be released from this heaviness. So, I keep walking...

However, the aisle to the altar is so long. The voice that yearns for me to be held captive by this weight whispers in my ear, *"Just turn around and go back. How are you going to kneel down with this basket in your arms? It is pointless to try and kneel.*

And if you could anyway it's not going to help. Do you honestly think that this basket full of pain is going to be instantly taken over when it is placed at the feet of Jesus?"

I answer the voice and reposition the weight that is straining my arms, saying out loud scripture from Matthew 11:28-30, *"Come to me, all who labor and are heavy laden, and I will give you rest. Take my yoke upon you, and learn from me, for I am gentle and lowly in heart, and you will find rest for your souls. For my yoke is easy, and my burden is light."* I quote the part of the scripture with every step, *"He said, 'My burden is light. Let me do the heavy carrying for you my child.'"* Just quoting it keeps me walking toward the altar to lay down the basket of burden that I know I can no longer carry.

I have come to realize that I am not able to carry these heavy burdens and this is why He has me here. He needs me to come to Him and present it as an offering, asking Him to take it. It is only then my doing this action that I will be freed from what is being held in my arms and the weight that is being exerted on my whole body.

As I continue down the aisle I realize I am only just a few more steps away from placing the basket at the feet of Jesus. It is then that the voices that want to stop me from reaching my destination become louder and louder. *"This is ridiculous, you honestly think that you can just place this at his feet and miraculously everything is going to be fixed? You are a dreamer. You are crazy. No wonder your family thinks you are nothing. No wonder you have all these problems. You are the failure."*

Yet, I keep walking. By this time, I am only a few steps away but that voice of hurt has caused the silent tears to trickle slowly and quietly out of the corners of my eyes and spill down my cheeks. Thankfully I feel the desperation of the hope welling up inside me to keep me going because I am holding to his promise that He has continuously told me through the years. I am reminded again of Psalm 55:22, *"Cast your burden on the Lord, and he will sustain you; he will never permit the righteous to be moved."*

Yes! I say to myself! That is right! That is why I am here! That is why I am making my way to this altar. For stronger reinforcement I say out loud, *"Get behind me Satan! The victory is already won and now that I have shown my God that I trust Him with every hurt, every burden and every bit of brokenness. He has already solved it all!"*

I lower the basket at the altar. It seems ironic because from what I think about is the day Christ was born and they knelt at his feet giving him adorning presents and here I am giving Him my troubles? That is not a present! Or...Is it? I am quickly reminded by His words in Ephesians 2:8 *"For it is by grace you have been saved, through faith—and this is not from yourselves, it is the gift of God—..."*

As I stay kneeling I say the word, *"My God, I need to give this all to you. I can't carry this anymore. I can't do it alone. But I know you gave your life to save my life and to make all things renewed."* It is in that moment I realize that I was able to make that walk because I first started in placing my hope that He could fix it all. Looking down at the necklace lying against my chest with the scripture of Philippians 4:13 *"I can do all this through him who gives me strength,"* reminds me that I can do it. Just to know those words were there to encourage me to keep walking and get to this place of giving it to Him. Now that I have placed it at His feet, I put my full trust in Him that He will now take care of it all.

I slowly rise off my knees and stand there at this altar realizing that my hands are now both free of debris. My shoulders are no longer hunched over from the burden. My back is able to stand more erect. My hands are open to be put to work.

> *"I removed the burden from their shoulders;*
> *their hands were set free from the basket."*
> Psalm 81:6

I look over to my right and I see a podium of where someone would stand and deliver a message from God. There is something on it but from where I am standing it is hard to make it out so I turn and walk towards it. As I approach the podium I see that it is a book that has been wrapped ever so beautifully in a gold ribbon inscribed with my name. I know it is a gift left for me.

"I never saw this before," I say. *"The podium and the gift were here the whole time I was walking my basket of burden down the aisle to place at the feet of Jesus?"* I am in awe. How could something so beautiful not have caught my eye? I hear the Holy Spirit speak into my heart, *"My child when you were burdened with what you were carrying you couldn't see anything but that. But now that you have turned it over to me you can see what I have been wanting to give you all this time. It was here at this specific spot just waiting for you. You see? You couldn't see it until everything was given to me. It freed you up to look see the gifts that I have already given you."*

I stood at the podium running my hands over this beautiful book and untied the gold ribbon. With my left hand, I open the page and there is a writing inscribed inside the front cover saying *"Go light the world my child. The words I give you have power to save lives and bring people to come to know me."*

I pick the book up off the podium and now bring it to my chest like a child does to a doll she loves so dearly. I stand there in awe, in solitude of what this journey has done for me for now I am light from the burden of pain and now reignited with the burden that I am to show others how to bring their baskets that hold them captive to the altar.

All because of my courage to walk; my endurance to keep on walking and placing my trust in Him has now reignited my hope and has reminded me to always trust Him for He will never fail me.

I pick up the book that has a pen attached with a gold cord and a cross at the end. I now have clarity of what I must do. And just to think...when I came into this little church carrying that heavy basket of struggle did I know the magnitude of my calling, my purpose.

With the book and pen in my left hand I raise both of my arms to the heavens and say with power. *"Thank you, God! Thank you for taking my burdens and replacing them with a new hope and a new assignment for Your Will."*

I now have a different walk leaving than I did when I arrived. I have lightness in my heart and a spring in my step. Yes, I do realize I have much to do. After all, He has called me to be a Warrior and a Warrior I must be. I can't FAIL to do what I now know I must.

The deep revelation comes to me that this would not have been revealed if I would have not surrendered to Him. I now walk heading out of the church singing:

All to Jesus I surrender,
All to Him I freely give;
I will ever love and trust Him,

In His presence daily live.

All to Jesus I surrender,
Humbly at His feet I bow,
Worldly pleasures all forsaken;
Take me, Jesus, take me now.

I surrender all,
I surrender all.
All to Thee, my blessed Savior,
I surrender all.

All to Jesus I surrender,
Make me, Savior, wholly Thine;
Let me feel Thy Holy Spirit,
Truly know that Thou art mine.

I surrender all,
I surrender all.
All to Thee, my blessed Savior,
I surrender all.

All to Jesus I surrender,
Lord, I give myself to Thee;
Fill me with Thy love and power,
Let Thy blessing fall on me.

All to Jesus I surrender,
Now I feel the sacred flame.
Oh, the joy of full salvation!
Glory, glory to His name!

I surrender all,
I surrender all.
All to Thee, my blessed Savior,
I surrender all.

Lyrics: Judson W. Van de Venter (1855-1939) Music: Winfield Scott Weeden (1847-1908)

As I sing this it causes me to ponder if these men in the 1800's knew how this song would impact millions of lives. That revelation causes me to clutch the gift of the book that God has placed in my hands as that is the legacy of delivering His glorious Word that will help the heart of another when it is needed.

STRATEGIES FOR IGNITING YOUR FIRE OF HOPE

1. Close your eyes and imagine all your worries, struggles, pain and fear. In your mind's eye see a basket and begin to load these into the basket as tangible items. What are the things that need to be placed in the basket? Why?

_____

_____

_____

_____

2. Now imagine your own walk to an alter where you know you must lay down this basket and freely give it to Jesus. What do you realize about yourself on this walk? How do you feel? What is the weight of all this and how is it affecting you?

_____

_____

_____

_____

3. You have reached the alter signifying that you are at the place where you can relinquish this basket over to Him. What are you saying to Him? What do you need to tell Him to help you feel released from these burdens?

_____

_____

_____

_____

4. Imagine standing up from the alter knowing that the burden is now carried by him and the heaviness as well as the anxiety of it has been removed from you. How do you feel now knowing that you have been freed from carrying all of this on you?

_____

_____

_____

_____

5. What clarity do you have now that you were not able to see or feel before this moment? What are some assignments that you know you must do to fulfill His purpose in your life?

_____

_____

_____

_____

SILENT TRIUMPHS

By Anna Brehm Anderson

SILENT TRIUMPHS

Hope is nurtured throughout life. It seeps into the fabric of our lives and helps define exactly who we are. When I was younger and kneeled at the bed to pray, my hopes were so simple. I hoped for a new doll or a new bike and I'm certain that not being a cry baby also was on my hope list. As we grow older, why is it so much harder to make hope a part of our lives? It shouldn't be a temporary fix to make one feel better.

"So, we fix our eye not on what is seen, but on what is unseen, since what is seen is temporary, but what is unseen is eternal."
2 Corinthians 4:18

Being raised in a large family has its merits and challenges. I am the third youngest of seven children. During my childhood and early adult life I was a CRY BABY! No matter how much I tried to contain my emotions, nothing ever worked. When I was away from my parents, I cried. Long distance telephone conversations with my sister always ended with me sobbing. Funerals were the worst because in addition to grieving over the loss of a loved one, the added anxiety of being so emotional was excruciating to me. I even tried counting the number of panes in the church's stained-glass windows in an effort to calm myself, but with no success.

I kept hoping one day I would discover a way to master my emotions. However, oddly enough this was only a trait that surfaced in my personal life. Professionally, I am focused, confident and successful. To my dismay, my mother once mentioned my *"softness"* to an employer and they were dumbstruck to think she was talking about me!

Over the years, I sought medical guidance and researched ideas, knowing it was crucial to control my emotions. Any new methods were put to the test with hopes they would allow my inward courage to approach personal situations with confidence – and with no tears! However, nothing ever stopped the emotional release. It was so embarrassing at times that I made excuses why I couldn't take part in events.

However, life changed dramatically for me in late 2002 when I discovered a walnut size lump during a breast self-exam. My first contact with the doctor's office was terrifying. My regular physician was off duty so I waited an additional day for an examination.

My physician explained the difference between lumps and cysts and asked if the area hurt. Of course, it did, I had been poking and prodding it for the past twenty-four hours. He confirmed it wasn't a cyst and scheduled a mammogram. The lump was not visible on x-rays. An ultra sound test was scheduled, but not for another week.

My husband, Lars, was away on a business trip and to make matters worse became stranded by an ice storm. We talked the night of my discovery, but I didn't mention the lump. I didn't want to worry him. Of course, Lars was upset later after he discovered that I decided not to tell him. However, I feel to this day, that I made the right decision. Afterwards we discussed the steps that should be taken and assured each other that together we could handle anything. Seven long days we waited, agonizing over what the possibilities could be and agreed this would be the last time we would put a diagnosis in a lengthy *"holding"* pattern.

The ultrasound confirmed the mass was *"suspicious,"* but no one uttered the *"C"* word. In my mind, I thought there was still hope. Then when the removal of the lump was discussed, the specialist used the *"I"* word. Unless the diagnosis was cancer, my *"INSURANCE"* carrier would not cover the surgery! Until now, I had stayed calm, listened to the prognosis and responded calmly to questions. But what I heard was we can't and won't help you! Did he believe I would live every day with the possibility of this lump becoming cancerous? I found myself raising my voice and became very accusatory, inquiring what route he would recommend for his own wife, daughter or sister in the same predicament. He left the examining room (I thought to call for security) but instead returned with an appointment to see a surgeon within the hour.

The surgeon had previously performed a medical procedure for me. I loved his sense of humor and was ecstatic that he would be my surgeon. We discussed my *"suspicious"* lump. I explained that my sister, Elizabeth, also had a breast cancer history. To be honest, I hoped my diagnosis would be the same as Elizabeth's, but that wouldn't be the case. My condition was much more advanced and the next critical step was a biopsy. Wow, I felt like a train had hit me. The surgeon took time to explain why a biopsy was so extremely important and assured me he would do everything in his power to remove the lump, but we needed to wait two very long days for the results. It was the Christmas season, my favorite holiday, and I found it increasingly difficult to go about my routine and find the spirit of the season!

Finally, when the doctor's office called, it wasn't the news that what we wanted to hear. The diagnosis was cancer and surgery was scheduled five days later. Lars and I discussed the diagnosis and the treatments and felt confident we had the best team available. We told our children and decided my sister, Elizabeth, should be the next to hear of my diagnosis. Then we talked with other family members before conveying the news to my elderly parents. Putting a voice to the cancer was harder than I had imagined, but discussing the diagnosis and treatments did become easier, that is until I had to tell my parents. This was the first indication that my crying had taken a backseat. No tears were shed as I explained my health issues. Looking them directly in the eye, with no emotion, I gave them the reassurance they needed.

My first surgery revealed that the cancer had spread to my lymph nodes. Two days before Christmas, I had my second surgery. Facing a diagnosis of stage III breast cancer, my treatments would be aggressive. Chemo and radiation treatments were ordered, with the promise of weight gain and hair loss, so I had that going for me! Gaining knowledge about my cancer was the first step of feeling in control. With my husband Lars at my side and one of the top oncologists in the country overseeing my treatments, I knew I could wage a darn good war against the cancer and I never looked back.

My Faith replaced any fears that surfaced and all my hopes were placed in God's hands. I knew God would give me the strength to maintain hope each day, to face whatever hurdles came my way, to guide the medical team in their decisions and provide strength for my family. I began journaling, encouragement resonated within my spirit – my hope! Eleven months after the initial diagnosis, two surgeries, nine months of chemotherapy and forty-five days of radiation along with adverse side effects, I was given the "OK" to begin the healing process.

When my physician said, *"How about we see each other in three months,"* I was thrilled. I began rebuilding my strength and getting on with my life, but in another sense, it meant that I was on my own, which was a very daunting, scary feeling.

How does one change their routine and mindset that quickly? Even though the appointments seem never-ending and all you want to do is get through them, it is difficult to step away from that regime. When a cancer patient walks through the clinic doors, he or she encounters instant smiles, positive reinforcement and attention. Everything is all about meeting the patient's needs and everyone's top priority is regaining healthy. It's a surrogate family that is always there. For eleven months, this was my life.

Depression began to creep into my *"new"* routine. Fortunately for me, I have a loving husband, children, family and friends who continued to monitor my progress and reinforced the belief that I was on the way to recovery. During this time, I searched out my battered journal and I realized throughout the entire ordeal my emotional crying had never surfaced. I had faced questions about life and death and heard the answers without a tear being shed. Why? What had occurred to manifest such a change? The very first journal entry provided me with my answer and has become one of my favorite verses: *"At times this life can beat us down with worries and sadness. When all seems hopeless, God's messages about hope can give us strength to take that next step forward – 'For I know the plans I have for you', declares the Lord, 'Plans to prosper you and not to harm you, to give you hope and a future.'"* Jeremiah 29:11

As the days turned into months and years, my diagnosis introduced me to many new cancer friends seeking answers to questions that only a cancer survivor can truthfully answer. My recommendation is to have confidence in care providers, consider a second opinion, and seek out family, friends and spiritual leaders. The most asked questions from my new cancer friends is how to find hope when cancer is waging a war in a person's body? Why me? What foods did you eat, were you tired, did you work? Is it possible to maintain intimacy in your life? At times, I just listened! I love this thought, *"Cancer is a rock in the path; step over it, the path will still be there."* It's true, I was fortunate, my life has continued on. When I reach out and help another woman over those rocks in her path, just as I was helped, I am a link in the chain that stretches from here to eternity — women helping women through breast cancer.

Through my illness, I am able to offer support to others, taking part in raising awareness through American Cancer Society events, as a guest speaker, raising funds, participating in annual runs, but most importantly I founded my company, *Silent Triumphs!*

These are my emotional and spiritual epiphanies as a Cancer Survivor: CANCER didn't conquer my Spirit, nor shatter my hope, nor corrode my faith! Cancer did not define me. I would find my true identity and be confident to step forward to be a positive example and voice for others. The healthcare professional can provide information for both emotional and medical support. Ask questions, learn and be honest! Bring another person to appointments and take notes. A second pair of ears is valuable when trying to understand an illness.

We move forward with our lives and sometimes find it easier to complain about the little things and forget about the small blessings in life. As my health progressively improved, my professional career and raising children became the focus. But death stops for no one! Within a span of little more than ten years, I lost my father, two of my brothers and my mother to serious health illnesses. However, I revel in the positives; and my sister, Patrica and brother Michael have remained cancer free.

We lost our father, Joseph Sr., to Multiple Myeloma Cancer two months after my final cancer treatment. One of my toughest conversations was discussing chemotherapy treatments with him. Though chemotherapy would have prolonged his life, he considered the quality of life to be unacceptable, and declined the treatments. My heart knew he would not survive. My hope was for him not to suffer.

My youngest brother, George, died from epilepsy complications. He was airlifted to a medical facility closer to family with a serious prognosis that was not life threatening. Unfortunately, within a few weeks he passed away from complications. It left us in denial and disbelief. Many times, I still feel as though I didn't do enough to save him. When those negative thoughts find their way into my daily routine, I read my battered journal: *"Do not dwell in the past, do not dream of the future, concentrate the mind on the present moment."* Buddha.

Another cancer tragedy arose when our brother, Joe Jr, was diagnosed with Stage IV Glioblastoma Brain Cancer. With surgery, chemo and radiation, his life expectancy was two to five years. My cancer experience made me the perfect choice for Joe's health advocate. We agreed to tackle his diagnosis and treatments together. WOW, why is our family so afflicted by cancer? The oncologist was reviewing the three sister's breast cancer diagnoses and it was apparent my file was of specific interest. We were told my breast cancer was genetically linked to my brother's brain cancer. Anxiety, fear, and a feeling of being overwhelmed instantly surfaced. It was important for me to be proactive in Joe's healthcare but I also had to deal with the knowledge that another cancer could return to attack my body.

Joe retired, and planned to travel the country after his treatments. Sadly, he passed away two months after his initial surgery. The hospital requested a wellness check when Joe missed an appointment and failed to answer the telephone. My instincts told me he was resting and dealing with the side effects of his treatments. However, Joe had died sometime in the previous thirty-six hours. The image of his body remains vivid; however, my experience that day was viewing a human being who was content, happy and most importantly, had a peaceful soul. Cancer cannot eat away or destroy the inner peace that comes from a spiritual presence.

Our mother, Mary, never knew of Joe Jr.'s passing. She was suffering through the late stages of dementia. Mom changed from an independent, faith-based, devoted wife and mother to a person with a personality change who didn't recognize us.

My emotional and spiritual epiphanies on losing parents and siblings: My parents are my role models. They had the ability to nurture seven very independent children to be strong and confident in their own identity. Though, being alone may be your choice, it may leave you vulnerable in your hour of need.

A friend is:
"A push when you've stopped
A word when you're lonely
A guide when you're searching
A smile when you're sad
A song when you're glad."

Everyone experiences life's lessons. I know that I am not alone. My journaling has continued to help me reflect when life isn't following my hopes and dreams. Family life can be difficult enough with biological parents and siblings, but when you blend a family, other circumstances enter into everyday life. Our children experienced periods of severe teen angst and difficulties in their early adult life. Their journey was filled with challenges, rebellion and disappointments! We butted heads on a regular basis. Tough parenting wasn't always the answer.

Some nights I would take refuge in bed, crying, feeling there was no hope and waking up to self-doubt with thoughts there was nothing I could do to help them. Then I realized that when deep doubts and fears surfaced, it diminished my Hope. You continue trying to make everything better because you are the parent. You provide unconditional love, and hope that by making things right, the situation will improve. However, change must originate with the individual. They must seek out help and guidance. My faith was continuously tested. These trials and tribulations were not meant to lessen my spirit but create a stronger spiritual bond. Our children have grown older and wiser and they now have children of their own to parent.

Lars and I are proud of our three children and the wonderful people they have chosen as partners — Ben and Sarah, Courtney and Justin, Eric and Melissa. We have twelve grandchildren — Samantha, Kyle, Odin, Lillian, Sophia, Liberty, Dylan, Nolan, Raegan, Jonah, Levi, Daemon, Griffin and Maelyn and a great grandson, Odin. Not a day passes that *"Gratitude"* isn't part of our thoughts and prayers. Our *"HOPE"* for our family is that their faith will carry them through life, and they continue to grow as loving and caring human beings.

Now and then childrearing conversations arise and we gently remind them of the times we questioned our parenting ability. But as parents, they need to continue to aim for those small victories and to remember life is a blessing!

Emotional and spiritual epiphanies from a parent: You question your parenting ability. Here's the simple truth—some kids are just more difficult than others. That is why it's so important to *"parent the child you have, not the child you wished you had."* At the end of the day, I believe God has placed me on hope's path and my faith will continue to guide me. *"Pray, and let God worry."* William Law.

Emotional and spiritual epiphanies of my life: Many of us who have faced life-threatening diseases have been given the *"Gift of Time."* Have we learned from our experiences or do we continue down the same path of self-destruction? Believe in something higher than yourself and you will never be alone! Cancer has strengthened my spirituality and led me down the path to create *Silent Triumphs! Silent Triumphs* is a collection of custom designed products to remind you how challenges can nudge you to reach outside your own known ability. The Illuminate jewelry product is shown reaching for a star and was created during my recovery from cancer and the simultaneous loss of my father. It was at this particular time, I experienced my first Silent Triumph, taking the time to appreciate and reflect and realize it is in our past, present and future challenges that mold our character.

From my early days of being that *"cry baby"* and stepping away from potential emotional situations to the present, when with my spirituality enables me to take part in life's situations. Hope should be embedded in your being! I am proud of myself, of where I am today, stronger and more carefree in life.

STRATEGIES FOR IGNITING YOUR FIRE OF HOPE

1. Are you doing what you believe in OR just doing to get by? And why would you just want to get by?

_____

_____

_____

_____

2. What stops your hopes from becoming reality? Hearing your words of hope out loud can make them feel within your reach.

_____

_____

_____

_____

3. What one single thing will you accomplish in the next 12 months that will matter in 5 years? Stop thinking the change has to come in one quick move.

_____

_____

_____

_____

4. What will be your legacy – how will you be remembered?

_____

_____

_____

_____

5. How can you offer hope to another person?

_____

_____

_____

_____

6. How do you enjoy your life every day? OR What consistently brings you joy?

_____

_____

_____

_____

ABOUT ANNA BREHM ANDERSON

Anna is an author, speaker, dreamer, sales professional and warrior who can find enjoyment in textile weaving or getting lost in a great mystery novel. She holds a degree in Hotel & Restaurant Management, is a Certified Meeting Professional (CMP) and a graduate of the Dale Carnegie Leadership Training and Disney's College of Knowledge.

As a Stage III Breast Cancer Survivor, Anna remembers her diagnosis and treatments as a time of feeling lost, intense anxiety and being terrified of all the uncertainty. Cancer changed her! By nurturing her spirituality, she grew stronger, was able her to express her emotions and gained inner strength to face life's challenges. The cancer diagnosis has placed her on a journey that she could never have imagined. She is reminded daily, to reflect on her accomplishments, recognize the strides she has taken and celebrate the successes of life, no matter how small.

Her company, *Silent Triumphs* came to fruition because of Anna's cancer diagnosis. Founding Silent Triumphs' offered her the chance to empower and encourage others to strengthen and build their own hope while facing life's challenges. Her first design, *"Illuminate,"* reminds the wearer, *"Sometimes you have to reach outside your grasp to grow inward."*

Anna resides in the Midwest with her husband, Lars, they have 3 children along with their spouses, 12 grandchildren and a great grandson.

Contact Anna:

- Website: www.SilentTriumphs.com
- Linked In: www.LinkedIn.com/in/anna-anderson-cmp-35a6b49
- Facebook: www.Facebook.com/SilentTriumphs
- Pinterest: www.Pinterest.com/SilentTriumphsLLC
- Email: Info@SilentTriumphs.com

MY GIFT OF INFERTILITY

By Desiree Anderson

MY GIFT OF INFERTILITY

My Infertility was a gift! How does that statement grab you? Are you tempted to say, *"How can you call a nightmare a gift?"* Once I listened to a sermon where the pastor proclaimed, *"Our devastations are a gift."* It made my heart physically ache. I felt my arms tingle followed by a sharp pain in my fingers. The pain was familiar. I experienced it every time I thought about wanting a child of my own.

For those who have dealt with the inability to become pregnant, not being able to carry a child to full-term, or the tragedy of losing a child at birth than the feelings of anger, sadness, emptiness and confusion become constant companions in your daily journey. They are unwelcome intruders in your life. How can one go from viewing pain as a burden to viewing it as a gift, and what happens during the journey? I asked myself these questions as I prayed, cried and found myself in a twilight zone that seemed to be an abyss of sadness. However, over time something inside my heart changed.

Why would I write about my sadness and share it with you? Why would I tap into the vulnerable part of my life and share my deepest hurt? Why would I allow you into my quiet place of suffering and brokenness? The answer centers on the metamorphosis that occurred during my journey, and a desire to share the joyful place of peace and hope I found on the other side. It's like Memaw's recipe for homemade macaroni and cheese. Once you try it and master the preparation phase, you want to share the secret. Soon others call to discover the blend of ingredients for the dish that makes Thanksgiving dinner so complete.

One day in my early 20's, a friend who was pregnant invited me on a shopping trip. As she was trying on maternity clothes, another friend and I decided to play with a maternity pillow to see what we would look like when we became pregnant. I studied my image in the mirror. A feeling of fear gripped me. I was at a place in my life where I did not want to become pregnant. My husband was frequently deployed, and the thought of raising a child without him frightened me.

I had a vision of a perfect family, with mom and dad home every night and at T-ball games on the weekend. This certainly wasn't the life of an Army wife. I wanted to wait until my husband would be home for a lengthy period of time, and

I completed nursing school. Basically, I told myself every excuse in the book why I shouldn't have children. And beyond the excuses I struggled with a small voice in the back of my mind that prepared me for the reality that I would never have a child of my own. I never shared those thoughts. I ignored them and continued the dialogue of *"not being ready."*

Life continued. I watched friends and family have children. Planning baby showers was one of my favorite pastimes. When a unit returned from Iraq, I sat at my coffee table, weekend after weekend, making corsages from tiny little blue or pink socks. I was happy for the parents-to-be and eager to volunteer free babysitting services.

Fast forward a few years. I was in nursing school attending an OB class when my instructor made a passing comment, *"Of course over thirty-five is advanced maternal age."* I blurted out, *"ADVANCED MATERNAL AGE!?"* She laughed. It hit me!! I was thirty-two and still had no plans to get pregnant. We had discussed trying to start after the next deployment. I realized I would be thirty-four when I got pregnant and thirty-five at delivery if all went according to plan. As the instructor outlined all of the potential complications for delivering at an *"advanced"* maternal age, I felt panicked.

Alas, the future did not go according to my plans. My first husband and I never had any children and I found myself in an unplanned and unwelcome paradigm of life that left me with many uncertainties. I had more questions than ever before. Answers eluded even the wisest people in my life. I was clinging to Jeremiah 29:11 which states, *"For I know the plan I have for you, declares the Lord, plans to prosper you and not to harm you, plans to give you hope and a future."* My future was already ordained and my hope was already solidified regardless of the current circumstances.

I met my new husband, John, a year later and we were married the following year. Although it was a bit soon, neither of us were getting any younger. We dedicated ourselves to family and the call of being parents. John had two children, Alex and Trinity. I could not ask for better, more loving children. We tried for five years to become pregnant. We had all the ups and downs that other couples have, complete with miscarriages, negative tests and hormone imbalances. It was an emotional roller coaster. Our efforts failed and we did not have any answers--just the perpetual question of, why?

We worked nights in the ICUs at the hospital and around July of 2013 I gained 35 pounds that came out of nowhere and would not budge. I had eaten what I thought was a clean diet and worked out my whole life but that no longer produced the same results. We dove into the true meaning of clean eating and how nutrition played a huge part in the ability to conceive a child. A company launched named IDLife that focused on Individualized nutritional supplements based on the latest research and that changed everything. My body finally had what it needed to balanced my hormones and my health was improving. We were Hopeful! When I changed to day shift after 9 years on night shift I got very sick, and after several weeks I finally gave in and went to see a specialist. I will never forget her words. She said, *"Well, as I look at your labs it is apparent why you were not able to conceive. Even if you had gotten pregnant, you would not have carried it to the second trimester, much less to full term."* So there it was. It had been 22 years since I was left alone in the dressing room at the maternity store with a pillow under my shirt and had my first glimpse of fear that I would never get to have a baby of my own. Now I heard it from someone who specialized in what was my current health status and she confirmed what had been placed in my heart many years earlier.

I went out to the parking lot and sat in my car watching the cars drive past. I felt broken. I wrapped my arms around my waist and squeezed. I felt as if I had a hole inside of me that could not be filled. My arms had ached for years to hold my own child, my stomach had longed to feel the movement of a baby inside of me and now somehow, I wondered why I was even alive. Why am I here? Why did the Lord put such a strong love in my heart for other people and for children if I was not have a child and be a mother? My mind was drawn back into my mother's kitchen where my mother, sisters and aunts talked of genealogy and how excited they were to have found my grandfather's little sister. I remember staring at the computer screen and seeing the web of children's names under each adult name. I envisioned my name many years from now being put into a genealogy search engine...but there would be no web. There would be no list of names. I cried for a while before I headed home but I wasn't lonely. I felt His comfort riding along with me on the hour-long drive back home.

Along the drive I was again reminded of the words I read many times in my life, *"For I know the plans I have for you."* He already knew my pain and he had already prepared me for what lay ahead.

As I dug into my faith and studied, I questioned myself. I questioned my motives and my heart. If I have dedicated my whole life to following the Lord, why then would I not trust His ways? Sometimes it takes painful disappointments to teach us who we really are, to teach us and refine the skill of truly trusting. Disappointments can strengthen faith if we allow. Disappointments also can position us to be in the right place to take advantage of opportunities that may not have presented themselves if the other door had not closed. We do not have to know His thoughts or His ways, but we are called to believe in His promise and His plan for our lives. I never felt sad at baby showers and was never jealous when someone told me they were going to have a baby. I always found a peace that this person whom I loved would not have to feel the same pain or sadness that I was feeling, and each time I thanked the Lord for sparing them of this heaviness. I found myself thinking, *"It's not about you, Desiree. It's not about you. It is not about your legacy."* I am called to live in such a way that when I die they do not put my name in a genealogy search engine. I am called to live a life of pointing others to Him. When they do a search, it is to find where they can find a hope that passes all understanding and that search will lead to Him.

First, I allowed myself to grieve. I needed time to mourn the loss of the children I would never carry. In Psalms 34:18 He says, *"The Lord is near to the brokenhearted and saves the crushed in spirit."* When I spent time in prayer I told Him that I was hurting and I asked Him to show me what I could learn from the pain. I learned to shift the focus to Him and away from me. I searched diligently for more ways to be a comfort to my patients during the brief time I was with them, and I learned to lean not on my own understanding. I learned to wait! Dear God in heaven, I learned to wait. Big things happen when we learn to wait and listen instead of trying to figure it all out on our own. Psalms 27:14 says, *"Wait patiently for the Lord. Be brave and courageous. Yes, wait patiently for the Lord."*

I learned to search for goodness. Seeking goodness during disappointment is one the hardest things to do, but I feel is one of the most necessary for development and growth in faith and personal development.

Years before I perfected the art of being sad and then picking myself back up and trudging on. When my first husband would deploy, I gave myself a twenty-four hour time limit to be sad. After that I would get up and get going. *"Suck it up butter cup!"* That was the phrase I said to myself and returned to a new normal.

This time I extended the time limit on sadness, but I made the decision not to allow myself to be consumed by grief. I wondered how I could miss someone I had never met so badly, but celebrated the freedom I found in being able to close that chapter in my mind and look to what His purpose was for each coming day.

"Weeping may last through the night, but joy comes with the morning."
Psalm 30:5

I learned a deeper meaning of believing in myself and believing in Him. It would be easy to let the enemy keep me in the thought process of *"not being good enough"* or *"being broken,"* but I knew I would never be effective for anything else in life if I allowed myself to be defined by those untruths. I knew my sadness was a part of His work and was preparing me for his ministry.

I searched the Bible for women who had been infertile and never had a child. I never found one. There are several who had trouble with conceiving but each was eventually able to have a child, and many times it was against all odds. So where did that leave me? It left me in the category of people who would be able to say, *"Lord, I will love you in the disappointment. I will love you in the midst of the pain and I will love you even if my prayers are never answered."* It left me in the category of people who get to celebrate Hope.

In the years to come John and I got custody of my great-nieces and great-nephews, and I became a parent to children who needed healing just as I did. My life is dedicated to being the best mother I can be for the six children who call our house their home. I spend my days parenting children who are energetic, enthusiastic and inquisitive, wounded and healing. We argue about appropriate clothing, when one should or should not start dating, and how to budget. I answer questions about diagramming sentences and algebra; I teach life skills such as cooking and doing laundry, drive children from point A to point B, drive to games and practices, wash skinned knees and even hit up the emergency department from time to time for broken limbs. John and I are committed to teaching the children to forgive other, to forgive themselves, to love others and to love themselves. We are committed to teaching them to love the journey of life and to embrace the disappointments as growing opportunities. We are committed to helping them learn to not be afraid of failure but to continue to do things that scare them and surround themselves with people who challenge them to grow. I do the job of a mother every day and I would not trade it for anything. I have the most amazing husband who is dedicated to being a father to children who are biologically his and ones who are not. He is right in the thick of it with me and we hit a high five as we tag-team while one enters the ring at home and the other heads off to work at the hospital.

You see, I am a mother; however, none of the children in my home call me *"Mom"*. They all have mothers who love them and I am thankful for those relationships. As part of my healing I had the names of my little girl, Isabella Prentiss Anderson and little boy, Gabriel Colton Anderson, embroidered on a blanket and buried them. It may sound morbid, but for me it was laying to rest a dream and a longing. It allowed healing and it allowed growth. It allowed a new day to begin.

My pain became my gift. I remember one time when I was a young child I heard my mother say, *"I wish I could keep all of my children from pain, but I would not want to rob them of the gift they will find when they discover their Hope in The Lord and that it will always be a constant."* I am thankful for the six children that were given to me to love and to teach. I am thankful in my role as their day-to-day mother. I have taught them all how to make Memaw's Mac and cheese. They have not replaced the children I was supposed to raise! They ARE the children I was meant to raise. The Lord was and is my Hope as I watch continue to watch him fulfill promise.

STRATEGIES FOR IGNITING YOUR FIRE OF HOPE

1. When you look at your life as a whole, what do you perceive is your main purpose for your existence? How are you living into that purpose each new day?

_____

_____

_____

_____

2. If you stay on your current trajectory where will you end up? Are you satisfied with the answer?

_____

_____

_____

3. Do you allow yourself to remain in a self-destructive state or do you choose happiness?

_____

_____

_____

_____

4. What have you learned about yourself from you past failures or disappointments? Have you allowed them to define you and your current states or have you used them as building blocks for personal growth and development?

_____

_____

_____

_____

5. Do you allow negative thoughts about yourself to take up residence in your mind or do you foster an environment of learning, growing and improving?

_____

_____

_____

_____

6. What metrics do you have in place to measure your growth and help you stay focused on your purpose?

_____

_____

_____

_____

ABOUT DESIREE ANDERSON

Desiree loves The Lord with her whole heart. She is a dedicated wife to John and a mother to Alex, Ashton, Trinity, Tyler, Kennedy and Daniel.

Desiree obtained her Bachelor of Science in Nursing from The University of Mary Hardin Baylor, and is a Nationally Certified Critical Care Nurse. She also held a Certification as a Sexual Assault Nurse Examiner {CA-SANE} for the Sexual Assault Prevention and Crisis Services Program for the State of Texas. She is currently transitioning from a career in Trauma and Emergency Nursing where she dedicated herself to caring for the physical, emotional, mental and spiritual needs of her patients to a career of serving others through coaching, speaking and mentorship. Her goal is to lead others to explore the extremities of their perception of themselves and to encourage personal growth as a continuing way of life. She helps organizational leaders understand and increase their leadership effectiveness and to create unique strategies for ministry teams, school systems and hospital administrators.

Desiree is a Certified John C. Maxwell Executive Coach, Leadership Trainer and Keynote speaker. Her goal in life is to leave a legacy for her children of making a difference, with people who make a difference, doing something that makes a difference at a time that makes a difference.

Contact Desiree:

- Website: www.CLPLI.com/Desiree_Anderson
- Email: Deskron613@gmail.com
- Email: DesireeAnderson@IDLife.com
- Phone: 706-577-3958

THEN THE PHONE RANG...

By Peg Arnold

THEN THE PHONE RANG...

"We also boast of our troubles, because we know that trouble produces endurance, and endurance brings God's approval, and his approval creates hope. This hope does not disappoint us, for God has poured out his love into our hearts by means of the Holy Spirit, who is God's gift to us."
Roman 5:3-5

I delighted in that sweet baby scent as I cuddled my newborn and nestled my nose in her neck. It was a taste of heaven! My spirit flooded with joyful gratitude for this new life that God had entrusted in my care. If only this moment could last forever.

Then the phone rang...

It was the pediatrician. I thought he was calling to check in on the baby, but that was not the case.

"Stephanie's blood tests have come back and we have some concerns."

My heart leapt to my throat. My precious daughter looked fine to me. She had a beautiful mellow complexion, which I quickly learned was a symptom of the problem.

"Her bilirubin count is dangerously high and we need you to bring her back to the hospital. She will need to be admitted immediately so we can put her under special lights and monitor her progress. If she does not improve, we could be looking at a blood exchange."

My mind was spinning. Take her back? Keep her for observation? Blood exchange? I was supposed to spend this time bonding with my newborn daughter-snuggling, nursing, bathing and sleeping.

With tear choked words, I tried to explain the details to my husband, Rick and my mother. I am sure I got the facts wrong, but I knew we immediately needed to get dressed, bundle Stephanie up and climb into the car for the forty-minute drive to the hospital. Mom attempted to reassure me, but the words *"blood exchange"* kept circling my brain and dominated my thoughts. Why was this happening?

When we got to the hospital, we went straight to the nursery from where Stephanie had been discharged, just hours earlier. Expecting them to admit her immediately, we were reprimanded by the nursing staff.

"You can't bring that baby in here! You need to report to pediatrics."

"What? Why," I cried. *"She was just discharged four hours ago and isn't even three days old yet! You have babies in there almost a week old and you're telling me she has to go to the area where sick children are?"* The thought of exposing my newborn to the germs that could be present in that unit frightened me.

"Absolutely," was the firm reply. *"Once a baby has been discharged, they are not allowed back into the maternity nursery."*

Now the mama bear came out, which surprised even me. *"You mean because I was strong enough to leave early, my baby can't come back? You are the ones who should have checked her earlier and not discharged her! I need to know what my options are and pediatrics is not one of them."*

After some reassuring words from a calm and understanding nurse, we arrived at a compromise. If I was willing to bring Stephanie in everyday for eight hours, they would allow her to receive the light treatment in a sterile room. In addition, they would send a special light home with us for her to sleep under every night until her bilirubin count was in a safe zone.

Little did I know the grueling process we were about to begin. Multiple blood tests, where they had to poke Stephanie's little heels and squeeze them so hard, only to extract a few drops of blood. Holding her while she screamed caused my milk to *"let down"* and soaked my shirt every time. Watching them wrap her face in this mask to protect her eyes from the light made it look like she was suffocating. My mom tried to put my mind at rest. Always the optimist, she pointed out the advantages of catching this condition right away. We were fortunate that Stephanie was getting the help she needed. She reminded me that she was praying for Stephanie to respond to the light therapy.

Did I have hope? Not quite! The fear was growing inside as the first blood test came back worse than the last. It seemed the treatment wasn't working. One more point higher and the doctor would prepare her for a blood exchange. A blood exchange! What might that expose her to? The option seemed too risky. Little did I know, God was building my endurance as this was only one of many challenging events I would face in the future.

Hope is like a faith muscle. To strengthen it, it is important to intentionally build endurance with scripture and focus on the gifts God reveals in the process. Stephanie was the answer to many prayers after many tests. My verse during this long arduous process of tests and temperatures, had been Hannah's song *"for this child I prayed."* Yes, what we went through was difficult, but we were blessed, as my daughter's condition was treatable and did not threaten her life. I didn't know how easily treatable her circumstances were in the process and instead, allowed my spirit to be controlled by the anxiety associated with the *"what ifs?"*

Throughout this challenging situation, I learned that I can protect my heart from the control of fear by focusing on the **Hope of God.** It took about a week, but Stephanie eventually did respond to the light treatment leaving only the silvery scars on her heels from the blood tests. It wasn't long before our lives settled into the routines and typical challenges associated with a newborn.

"For I know the plans I have for you," says the Lord. *"They are plans for good and not for disaster, to give you a future and a hope."*
Jeremiah 29:11

It was May, twenty-two years later, that the season of graduation hit our family in duplicate! Both of my children were graduating; one from high school and the other from college. It was busy and stressful, but also exciting, as we planned for all of the celebratory events. There were out-of-state travel plans to make for Stephanie's graduation from college. This included transportation, lodging, meals and even a celebratory family banquet. Simultaneously, I was completing invitations for our son's high school graduation and open house. There was so much to do, but all very exciting. I felt like I was surfing on a curling wave of anticipation.

The weekend in Michigan for Stephanie's college graduation went smoothly. It was a whirlwind of events filled with family time and proud moments captured in memorable pictures. To top it off we were celebrating a third-generation graduate from Western Michigan University! It was a true legacy moment, a memory captured in pictures that would be treasured in our hearts forever.

As soon as I returned to Maryland, I had to jump right into the roller coaster of events for my son's high school graduation. Preparations for the arrival of two sets of grandparents coming from out of state needed to be made. Where would everyone sleep? Pick-ups from the airport needed to be arranged, tickets reserved, not to mention the meal planning. We were so excited to have both sides of the family join us for all the festivities, from baccalaureate to open house to the commencement ceremonies. This would only be the third time we had all been together since my husband and I got married. With my parents in Michigan and his parents in California, family gatherings did not happen often in our Maryland home. This celebration however was going to be another legacy moment creating that picture and memories that we would cherish for a lifetime.

Then the phone rang...

This was the first crack in this legacy painting that I created in my mind. It was my dad calling from Michigan. I knew by the sound of his voice that the news would not be good. My Dad, a cardiac patient, had been healthy for years, but a recent visit to the doctor revealed a new blockage, requiring surgery. He assured me that this was not life threatening, but necessary. The difficult news to hear was that it had to be scheduled at the Cleveland Clinic and the only opening they had was during the week of my son's graduation.

Of course, I was extremely disappointed that my parents would not be able to celebrate with us. The picture of eight was now reduced to six. We would miss them greatly, but my mom and dad were where they needed to be and God was in-charge. I knew there would be more opportunities for more legacy moments in the future for our families to celebrate together.

The week of graduation grew near and we were making final plans for each event; cleaning the house, manicuring the gardens, purchasing decorations, food items and more. We were in count-down mode and planning to pick up my in-laws at the airport the next day.

That morning began as any other, drinking coffee and reading my devotions on the back porch.

Then phone rang...

My husband answered the call and it was clear by his voice that something was very wrong. I walked out to the kitchen, just as he hung up the phone, *"It's my dad,"* he said, *"he had a massive heart attack, he...did not survive."*

It was as if someone had ripped our lives right in half. This wasn't supposed to happen! My father-in-law never had any cardiac issues and he was only seventy years old! The shock was paralyzing. The chance to share a legacy moment with both sets of parents in the future was lost forever. Instead of picking up my husband's folks from the airport that morning, we were thrown into a cyclone of decisions and grief. Does my husband leave to be with the family and his Mom? Do I go with him? What about the baccalaureate? What about the open house? What about graduation? Not to mention, how do we afford last minute cross-country airline tickets?

We decided that this was one of those situations where we needed to divide and conquer. My husband would leave to be with his family and I would stay home so that my son could participate in all his graduation events. Nothing felt celebratory. Instead it felt like a dark cloud was shadowing everything. I kept thinking, *"for the Lord has plans for you plans for good and not for disaster, to give you a future and a hope."* Where was the good? Where was the hope?

When things like this occur, hope seems out of reach. Everything in my immediate vision blocked any sign of hope, yet I knew God was there, somewhere. I started searching for an airline ticket for my husband. How long would he be gone? Would he miss everything with our son? My son was feeling as if his own graduation, which should be a high point in his life, was now just a big inconvenience to everyone. We all wanted to go to California but the cheapest ticket was $650 one way! It was completely unthinkable, let alone possible. Where would we get the money for just one person to go?

Then the phone rang...

It was a dear friend who heard about our loss through our church's prayer chain notice about Dad's death. She was calling to see what she could do and without me saying anything she said, *"We have airline points and could get your husband a ticket if that would help!"* I had tears of gratitude as I remembered God's promise and plans. This was His way of providing Hope in the midst of a devastating loss, assuring us that we were not alone.

It wasn't long before my friend worked her magic to purchase the airline ticket with her points. Instead of driving to the airport to pick up my in-laws, I was kissing my husband good-bye and dropping him off to fly west to be with his mom and family. Our instructions were to stay home for the graduation events, until final plans were made. It happened that there were two grandchildren graduating that week and my mother-in-law did not want either one to miss their commencement ceremonies. She had made the decision to cremate my father-in-law and schedule the memorial at a time when it would not conflict with the other events. In addition, it give more lead time allowing families to buy more affordable airline tickets. This was another sign of God's plan for hope in a time of devastating loss.

I returned home to get ready to attend the baccalaureate with my son and daughter. We had eight tickets and now we only needed three. I was not prepared for the wave of emotion that hit me as I handed in the unused tickets. It was another confirmation that this was a permanent hole in our family and there would be no more celebrations with Grandpa. I tried to keep a cheerful demeanor but it seemed all the graduation events were now shadowed with this huge shroud of loss and grief. Not only did we not have any grandparents at the baccalaureate or open house, but my husband was absent as well.

In spite of all the sadness and disappointments, we celebrated as much as we could together and were excited to find out that my husband would able to return for the actual graduation day. To make the day extraordinary, we invited dear family friends to attend the graduation ceremonies and a celebratory lunch. I was determined to embrace the day, getting up early to make a special breakfast for the family.

Then the phone rang...

My husband answered it upstairs so I had no idea who called. When he came downstairs, I instantly knew something was wrong.

They say things always happen in threes, and here was the third event that cracked the happy graduation day picture I had envisioned. My husband told me that it was his boss, calling to inform my husband, over the phone, that his position was eliminated, effective, immediately. Yes, I mean his job, fired, over the phone, the same week his father died! No real reason was given except *"reorganization."* His boss said that he would be expected to turn in all keys, car and company belongings the next day.

I couldn't believe my ears and thought he was kidding. I said,

"This is a joke, right?" Thinking there is no way this could be happening, not now, not this. He assured me it was not a joke.

"Did he know your dad just died?"

"Oh yes, he even said before hanging up, 'oh by the way, sorry about your dad,'" he said.

"Did he know it is your son's graduation day?"

"Not sure, and I wasn't about to tell him."

I was livid, dazed, grieved, all at the same time. But something happened right at that moment. You can call it crazy, but I call it, Hope, God's hope. I looked tearfully into the eyes of my husband. We embraced each other and danced. Danced right there in the middle of the kitchen, just the two of us, crying and swaying while I sang, *"Bend me break me any way you want to, long as you love me, it's alright!"*

Solomon was very wise when he penned, there is a time for everything: *"a time to weep and a time to laugh, a time to mourn and a time to dance"* Ecclesiastes 3:4. Sometimes in the midst of grief and mourning, the best way to feel Hope is...to dance.

Hope, God's hope, doesn't come to you as a gift with decorative wrappings and pretty bows delivered with excited anticipation. Most of the time, God's Hope is like a treasure hidden in the murky dark places where fear resides, grief overwhelms and worry abounds. Earthly eyes will only see the negative possibilities, the impossible hurdles and the harmful obstacles. If we wallow in our challenges allowing them to monopolize our focus and thoughts, hope is easily lost.

Sometimes hope is a little light in the darkness. Sometimes it is friend's compassion and support that exposes the treasure of hope. Sometimes it is the words of scripture that pierce through the murky mess giving you confidence that God is in control. Never give up in seeking out the treasure of God's hope when circumstances seem overwhelming and impossible. The answer may not always be what you want, but you are never alone in the midst of the storm.

"We also boast of our troubles, because we know that trouble produces endurance, endurance brings God's approval, and his approval creates hope. This hope does not disappoint us, for God has poured out his love into our hearts by means of the Holy Spirit, who is God's gift to us."
Roman 5:3-5

The season of grief is a difficult one. We survived that graduation day, but not without tears and missing the presence of our family members. We eventually were able to grieve the loss of my father-in-law and celebrate his life with extended family but things did not return to normal. God continued to build our muscles of endurance through the challenges of lingering grief woven together with the trials of unemployment.

We experienced hope when my husband saw his joblessness as an opportunity to help his mom clean out, organize and down-size. This gave him chances to witness to his family and help his Mother process her grief. However, it did involve extensive travel, leaving me alone quite often.

One of those weekends when I was home by myself, I was outside consumed with gardening.

Then the phone rang...

It was my dad and mom calling together. My dad had come through his heart surgery with flying colors, but now mom had been going through a number of tests and they had just received the news. When I asked what the results were,

"I'll have your mom tell you," my dad said.

"Mom?" I said inquisitively.

There was a pause and then with an unsteadiness in her voice, she replied, *"It's that disease... oh how do you say it, ...Alzheimer's?"*

> *"Don't be afraid, for I am with you. Don't be discouraged, for I am your God.*
> *I will strengthen you and help you. I will hold you up with my*
> *victorious right hand."*
> Isaiah 41:10

Hope...

STRATEGIES FOR IGNITING YOUR FIRE OF HOPE

1. Do you have a time when a call or text shook your life?

_____

_____

_____

_____

2. Have you ever felt you had worked through a challenge and then were blind-sided with the grief?

_____

_____

_____

_____

3. In what ways have you found hope in the midst of heartbreak or fear?

_____

_____

_____

_____

4. How has hope changed your view of a crisis?

_____

_____

_____

_____

5. What Hope signals can you identify when you get on the other side of a challenge?

_____

_____

_____

_____

6. When you're in the midst of a challenge, what blinds you from Hope?

_____

_____

_____

_____

ABOUT PEG ARNOLD

Peg Arnold has a passion for encouraging women to find their true value and purpose. As a leader in women's ministry for more than 25 years, Peg's positive messages and fresh approach makes scripture come alive as it is woven together with personal witness, drama, teachings and humor. Through her writings and presentations, she inspires and encourages all to embrace and accept Christ's love and empowers them to use their gifts in their daily lives. She is a firm believer that we all have value in the Body of Christ!

As a wife, Mom, Nana, sister and friend, she has been an active prayer warrior and leader in her church and community. She loved her 30 years of teaching and counseling in Maryland schools while balancing that with serving in her ministry opportunities. Peg and her Soul Mate - Rick have recently relocated to Colorado to spend more time with their family.

Whether it's sharing over a cup of coffee, on a walk, studying in a group or participating at a conference or retreat, she loves to encourage others as they seek God's direction in life's joys and challenges.

Contact Peg:

- Website: www.PegArnold.org
- LinkedIn: www.LinkedIn.com/in/Peg-Arnold-64803616
- Facebook: www.Facebook.com/PegArnoldWOW
- Facebook Videos: www.Facebook.com/groups/1695865280710398
- Twitter: www.Twitter.com/ArnoldPeg
- Instagram: www.Instagram.com/ArnoldPeg
- Pinterest: www.Pinterest.com/WonderOfWomen
- Email: PegArnoldWOW@gmail.com

RESCUED

By Kate Bancroft

RESCUED

As I got out of the car, I saw Willie for the first time. He was across the yard in a small corral. I could see he was skinny, dirty and looked sick. So many thoughts were swirling in my mind. Hesitating, I looked around thinking this cannot be the horse I came here to see. I turned to my friend, who was responsible for me being there, to tell her that this was not going to work. I then realized that Tori, my daughter, was already out of the car and running towards him. This is not what I had in mind!

My friend, who runs a horse rescue, called me because she knew I had space for a horse. She had received a call about an Appaloosa and a draft horse. Both were in a rough place and needed a new home. She had run out of space at the rescue and couldn't take them in. I immediately passed on the draft. Much bigger than I wanted to handle! She told me the Appaloosa was a bit thin and asked if I would go look at him with her. You know how you get a picture in your mind how something is going to look? That's what I did, I pictured a big beautiful horse that just needed a few groceries. It was almost romantic, I would get to be a knight in shining armor and rescue the damsel in distress. Only reality didn't line up with my vision of Willie. Every rib, vertebrae and hip bones were visible.

Crossing the yard to the corral Willie was in, well, let's just say he looked much better at a distance. No, I just have to say no. (Yes I was repeating it over and over!) He is too skinny, too far gone and much more work that I want to sign up for. How do I get out of this mess? My friend is telling me about his past and how he wound up here. A retired champion barrel racer? Really? All I could see was an old broken down bag of bones whose time is up. Tori is calling me into the corral to meet him. Are you kidding me?! Get out of there! Everyone knows you don't pet the puppy because the puppy will come home with you and you should NEVER bring your 11 year old daughter, who loves every animal, especially horses, to look at a horse that needs to be rescued! I ran my hand over his hip and am struck by how tight his skin is over his bone and how rough his coat feels. I do not want to take him home. He is not my problem. He is too far gone. Just say no and walk away. Then it happened. Tori, my little girl with a heart the size of Texas, threw her arms around his neck to give him a hug and Willie, closed his eyes, laid his head on her shoulder and sighed. It was the sigh that changed my life. She turned to me with tears in her eyes, eyes that were imploring me to give this guy a chance, to bring him home.

I love how God takes our everyday encounters and shines scripture on them. A rescue facility had no room for a rescue? This was where Willie should have gone, a place with the knowledge and experience to handle a case like his. At that season of our lives, if we had applied to adopt a rescue from an agency, I believe we would have been turned down. Sometimes our plans get turned upside down. There was no room for Joseph and Mary at the Inn. That is where Jesus should have been born. God's ways are far above ours. Often, we don't see His hand in things until after we walk through them. I am sure Joseph was not too pleased at the prospect of his wife giving birth in the stable. Yet, that is exactly where He was supposed to be born. Jeremiah 29:11 *"'For I know the plans I have for you,' declares the Lord, 'plans to prosper you and not to harm you, plans to give you hope and a future.'"* His plan is to give us hope and a future. We definitely do not understand or see all that God is doing behind the scenes in our life.

The whole family was in the yard to welcome Willie to his new home. I did warn my husband about how thin Willie was but words just do not prepare you for the live version. The trailer ride to our house was difficult. Willie was weak and had a nasty fall on his trip. The look on my husband's face as he came out of that trailer said it all. We were now the caregivers to a 23 year old, skinny, sick Appaloosa gelding with a major wound on his leg from his fall. There was so much we did not know, that we needed to learn. I had never cared for a *"special needs"* horse before. *"Is he going to survive the winter?"* was all my husband said. The only answer I had was to shrug my shoulders because I really didn't know. As I watched the trailer pull away, the reality of what we just did set in. Willie was now *"my problem."*

You cannot just throw a bunch of food at a person or an animal that has been starved. I never understood why the programs that feed starving children give them a dish of porridge. Give them something with substance! In the two weeks it took to bring Willie home, we learned all we could about how best to care for him and what to feed him. He wasn't like the other horses that we could just toss hay to. Everything he ate had to be monitored. If we gave him too much, too soon, we could really hurt him. We started with nutrient dense *"mash,"* small portions, a few times a day. It didn't take him long to realize that my husband had good stuff in that bucket for him! He quickly became the family favorite, we all had our hand in this *"Rescue Willie"* project! He patiently stood through all of his treatments as if he realized that he was safe at last.

Recovering from starvation takes time. Time was not on our side, winter was fast approaching and we were concerned how he would handle the cold. Again, seeking how best to help him, we made the decision to blanket him. He was on the mend and I was no longer worried about someone reporting us for animal abuse because of how he looked. We endured plenty of negative looks and comments from people driving by when we had him out in the yard. Glimpses of his true personality, the one that made him a champion barrel racer, began to emerge. He was coming back to life. One day, watching the horses run in the pasture, I fixated on Willie. It was like a slow motion scene in a movie (cue music). He was running and throwing up clumps of dirt behind him, the sound of his hooves hitting the ground was like thunder. Imagine a wild stallion running free...well, minus his blanket. The other horse with him is fast but was quickly left behind. What power and speed he had! It was the first real moment of his true self. I saw him differently after that. Seeing past the hurt, sickness and abuse to seeing his heart.

As winter progressed, Willie continued to improve. The hope that Tori had was coming true. I began to believe it too. The connection between Willie and my son deepened. With myself and my daughter, he acted like his barrel racer self. All confident and proud. But with Kegan, he was quiet, patient and would stand for hours while he was brushed. Kegan's confidence grew and by spring he had taken over Willie's care. I love Spring. The promise of new life. Of course, the warmer weather. We emerged from winter victorious! Willie not only survived the winter, he was beginning to thrive.

Summer brought hours of fun with the horses. It brought us a picture of how Willie was in his prime. He was beautiful and he knew it! His coat glistened in the sun and he was a picture of health. While riding him in the arena, Tori discovered just how fast he could turn a barrel. So fast, he almost left her behind. I think they both enjoyed the fun. Kegan, fully confident in Willie, began practicing his riding skills. He worked diligently all summer to get himself and Willie ready for the fair.

The leaves were turning, reminding us that seasons change. Willie became ill. The vet came and antibiotics were given. A few days later, the vet was back with different medication. This went on for a week before it looked like we turned the corner. He had lost a lot of weight but was back to his playful self. We all took a deep sigh of relief. That was short lived. The next night he had a massive stroke and was gone. We buried him on the farm with a hand painted marker. Holding my son after, trying to comfort him in his grief, he held up Willie's halter and said this is all I have left of him.

In total, we had Willie in our lives for 15 months. I often said that we gave Willie the best last year of his life and felt good that we helped him. Often with God, you don't see how He is at work until afterwards. We brought Willie home to help him. To give him a future and hope. Not once did I think, *I wonder what God is going to do in us through Willie?* Isn't that how God works, behind the scenes in the unexpected places. We are still impacted by what we learned because of him today.

I am reminded of what the Lord told Samuel when meeting David's brothers ,1 Samuel 16:7 *"But the Lord said to Samuel,"* '*Do not look at his appearance or physical stature, because I have refused him. For the Lord does not see as man sees, for a man looks at the outward appearance but the Lord looks at the heart.'"* When I first met Willie, I judged him on his appearance. At the end of his life I was still judging Willie's health by how he looked. The damage done to his internal organs because of being starved was unseen. Many times I look at someone in their brokenness and don't try to see deeper. I am stuck on the outward just like I was with Willie. He was hopeless to change his situation, he needed someone to reach out and hope for him. Can I see as God sees, past the sin and shame, the brokenness and pain, and extend the Hope I have in Jesus to them? In Acts 3:4 *"and fixing his eyes on him, with John, Peter said"* '*LOOK AT US.'"* They noticed this man who had been sitting, begging at the gate for most of his life. How many people walked by him daily and never saw him. Peter and John tell this man that which he is asking for isn't what they have and isn't what he needs. In verse 6, Peter tells him *"what I do have I give you, In the name of Jesus Christ, rise up and walk."* This man is only hoping for money but is given so much more. The hope that is Jesus.

We were looking for a companion for Tori's horse. Something cheap and easy. What we were given was Willie. Certainly not cheap or easy! Hindsight allows us to pull back the curtains and get a glimpse of why Willie came to us.

Willie brought with him unity for our family. We were all committed to caring for him. We were all working together for the same goal. His health and wellbeing.

Willie opened communication between us. He was an easy conversation starter. *"Guess what Willie did today?"* was common at the dinner table.

Willie gave Kegan a sense of belonging. He had just had a rough patch with friends and he really needed the security and acceptance. Kegan was helping Willie heal and it seemed like Willie knew Kegan needed healing also.

Willie gave Tori and Kegan common ground without competition and to learn how to have fun together. With Tori, he was the champion barrel racer. With Kegan, he was a gentle giant.

Through Willie, we served without any question of getting something in return. We learned to celebrate the small victories. Each day he made it through mattered, what we did for him was worth something.

When I first met Willie, I had NO hope, NONE, for his recovery. I must have heard a gazillion times growing up *"Don't get your hopes up."* My lack of hope was tied to not being disappointed. If I hope and it doesn't work out then there is pain so maybe I just shouldn't hope. In Proverbs 13:12, we are told that hope deferred makes the heart sick. So could my lack of hope be called a heart condition? Even though I had seen many incredible things God had done in my life, I think the scared, hurt little girl inside me had put hope in a box and shoved it under the bed. Tori just wanted to give Willie a chance. She just wanted to try. She kissed him on the nose and said *"I hope he is going to be all right."* The thought in my head was *"Well he is just going to die."* That is not what I wanted to tell my 11 year old daughter! Having no hope, I attached my hope to Tori's and said *"Me to."* Sometimes, all you have is someone else's hope. You've got to stand on their belief until you are able to stand on your own.

Hope is a difficult word. We use it so often it seems diluted. *"I hope I get the job." "I hope it doesn't rain." "I hope the Lions win."* It's becomes a word to reflect how we want a situation to happen, not a word to reflect the Hope of Jesus Christ. Restoration of our hope isn't about changing our attitude. It's about changing our vision. Nebuchadezzar threw Shadrach, Meshach and Abednego into the furnace. Their situation looked hopeless but they didn't focus on the situation they focused on the One who is their Hope.

Psalm 23 is read so often at funerals that it is commonly called the *"death psalm"*. I want you to read this out loud and listen, really listen. Psalm 23: 4, *"Even though I walk through the darkest valley, I will fear no evil for You (GOD!) are with me."* Right there, in the midst of our deepest, darkest moments, God is with us. Emmanuel, means With us God! His hand upholds us. His love surrounds us. His peace is held open like a big, warm blanket ready to wrap around us.

We lose sight of this in the trials of life. Distracted by the pain of loss. Loss seems like the big, dark hole that sucks us in, saps our strength and steals our hope. So how do we take the step back to hope?

Something I learned from someone very wise is this...

"What we focus on we find." "What we focus on expands." "What we focus on we become."

What is our focus? We focus on Jesus and that through Him we find hope, truth, love, forgiveness, healing, grace, mercy and salvation.

What we are focusing on now expands! Our hunger for Jesus grows, a deeper relationship develops and transformation happens!

We are now in the process of becoming! It is no longer I who live but Christ lives in me! We are sowing, tending and harvesting for His kingdom. We are ready to give an answer for the Hope within us! All because we began to focus on our true Hope, Jesus Christ.

I read an acronym for hope that said, *"Hold on pain ends."* I don't think that sounds like hope at all, to just hang in there until you get through. How many times have I tried to get through something on my own strength? Far too many. It's no wonder I fell flat on my face. I came up with my own. Well, I didn't like any of my *"o"* words so feel free to add your own, Holiness Promises Eternity. He doesn't promise an easy ride. He promises He will never leave us to walk through it alone. He promises that Jesus is our Hope.

Willie has been gone for 12 years and as I was sharing his journey, I cried. The *"why"* of God bringing him into our lives is still being felt. This horse taught us so much about courage, endurance and hope. He left behind much more than his halter.

Hope, love and loss mixed together making our hearts softer for the broken of this world and stronger to live our life on the frontlines for Jesus Christ.

STRATEGIES FOR IGNITING YOUR FIRE OF HOPE

1. Is there a time in your life that you lost hope? How did you walk through it?

_____

_____

_____

_____

2. How do you see the people begging on the side of the road? Do you help them? Why?

_____

_____

_____

_____

3. Read Jeremiah 29:11. Make a list of all the ways God has given you a future and hope.

_____

_____

_____

_____

4. In what ways to you judge people by how they look?

_____

_____

_____

_____

5. What you focus on you find. What are you focusing on?

_____

_____

_____

_____

ABOUT KATE BANCROFT

Kate Bancroft understands how to turn your weaknesses into strengths. Kate develops growth, brings hope and trains women who are fighting the giants of self-limiting beliefs and the food they use to mask the pain. She is committed to walking with these women on their journey to breakthrough. She celebrates that when a giant falls, the true treasure they are is revealed. Kate draws from her 30 plus years in ministry, customer service, business building and life experiences to impact and transform lives through her coaching, speaking and writing. Her retreats and workshops provide a space to discover the weapons needed to fight and win against the giants in your life.

Kate is certified through The John Maxwell Team as an Executive Leadership Coach, Personal Growth and Development Coach and Communications.

Kate is a recovering chocoholic and an eating disorder diva who lives down a little dirt road with the love of her life, her husband Brian.

Contact Kate
- Website: www.SlayingGiantsWithKate.com
- Facebook: www.Facebook.com/Kate.Bancroft.94
- LinkedIn: www.LinkedIn.com/in/Kate-Bancroft-967559104
- Email: Kate@SlayingGiantsWithKate.com

UNREASONABLE HOPE - BEYOND WHAT CAN BE ACCEPTED

By Wendell Betts

UNREASONABLE HOPE - BEYOND WHAT CAN BE ACCEPTED

Hope! What is hope and where does it come from? Hope is one of the most used words in the English language, or any language for that matter. How many times have you thought, *"I hope my day goes well. I hope my car starts or I hope I get that new job?"* Do we use the word hope too lightly? Probably so, right along with the word love.

Hope takes strength and must be applied like faith. Hope requires action. One can have never-ending hope, but without action hope is essentially useless. It is much like waiting for a car to start without placing the key in the ignition.

Hope can grow or it can be lost. The final decision belongs to you. Hope can be snatched away through a bad word or report, or instilled in your heart.

I have my own story about hope. It began in March 2013. I was sitting with my pulmonary physician having the conversation that no one wants to have, especially when it is about you. It's a place where everyone arrives eventually. I asked the questions, *"Where do I go from here and what should I expect next?"*

Dr. Williston pulled her chair close, looked at me straight in the eyes and lovingly said, *"Wendell, I cannot say how long you have but with your history and the condition of your lungs, all I can say is that the next time you get sick one of two things will happen; you will either be intubated (put on a breathing machine) or you will die. With your past medical history and where you are now I cannot guarantee you thirty, sixty or ninety days."*

As my mind began to comprehend the reality of the diagnosis I said to Dr. Williston, *"Then I am going to die because I am not going on a machine to keep me alive. That is not living. I want you to put DNR on my medical report."*

She advised me to go home and have a talk with my wife, Sharon, and my family. I wondered on the way home, *"How do you tell the ones you love such devastating news?"*

At this point you're probably asking where do you find hope in this? How do you keep a positive mindset when medical authorities advise that you may not have ninety days to live? Where is your hope now? Even if you live life with a positive outlook, when the message is this bleak most are tempted to give up. Not me. I am a warrior. I refuse to quit. It isn't in my DNA. I have never quit, and I never will.

As I left the physician's office, I told myself, *"You do not have the power to tell me when I am going to die or how many days I have left on earth. Only God knows how many days I have been given."* I vowed to fight with all that was within me. I was determined not to become a mere number or statistic.

As I drove home that morning my thoughts recalled a Saturday in August 2012 when I had slipped to my lowest point ever. I simply did not want to go on. On that hot, humid rainy day I told God that it was easier to die than to live. God had a clear, decisive answer. He said He *"could do more with what was left of me than I ever did with the best of me,"* and promised to use my life to influence a multitude of people.

I took hold of this and stood fast to what God told me that day. Therein is my HOPE. My hope comes from the Lord. I trust in Him and Him alone.

With that in the forefront of my mind and believing in my purpose, I continue to fight and walk on. *"When the world around you is in a dilemma and most are overcome with fear and ask the question, where do we go from here? You will be half way there just by this one simple task; walk on."* — from Andy Andrews' book *The Noticer.*

Choose to embrace life, and let the universe know that you don't intend to don your pajamas, lie down and wait for death to come. When you decide not to quit, things will and do happen for the better.

Within two months after committing to the fight, my wife Sharon and I met an old friend at a church service. Neil operates a health and wellness clinic in the city where we live. He is very good at what he does. Neil came to me after the service and said he wanted to help. I told him my financial situation wouldn't support his services. He said, *"No Wendell, that is not what I mean. I need to help you. I want to help you."* He gave me his business card and told me to call the following Tuesday to schedule an appointment.

The friend who initially invited us to the church service was present as well. Spencer Court owns a gym, and invited us to use it on an unlimited basis.

This is how the universe answers you back when you put it out there that you are willing to be the best you can be, and have the desire to become more. Hope mixed with faith and a positive mindset is a powerful force. Add the never quit attitude and it is a recipe for ultimate success.

At this point my hope started to grow and my faith strengthened. This was a momentum builder. I weighed over 360 pounds, the largest I had ever been. I called Neil that Tuesday and met with him later that week. He didn't charge me for his service. He said as long as I was willing to follow his plan of action he would continue to help me. Did he ever help! He opened my eyes about food and nutrition and what I should eat. He changed my way of thinking about food. From May through August I adjusted my eating habits and lost thirty-five pounds. We also visited the gym two or three times a week. I would hit the treadmill for three to five minutes and then go home and recover for the next twenty-four hours to gain the strength to go back for another three to five minutes again. During these times at the gym I carried my oxygen tank, cranking it up to five, the highest setting. I was determined. My hope would not let me quit.

By August Sharon and I were in a desperate place. We had put our home up for sale and knew we were only ninety days from losing everything. We even talked about walking away and letting the bank foreclose. Our savings were completely gone. This is where hope and faith come to be, hope that needs will be met and a miracle is on the horizon along with faith that God will provide. During this time, we learned that God's ways are not our ways and His timing is always perfect. When praying for a miracle we must be open to His ways. Be ready to accept the miracle He puts in front of you. It probably will not look like you thought it would. Open your mind and allow Him to work.

Point in case. In August 2013, a couple who frequently visited and prayed with us left some samples of gourmet coffee and mentioned a sales opportunity. We tried the coffee and enjoyed it. A few days later we called the number on the business card the couple had left with us. We were invited over for coffee and to take a look at what they had to offer. Up to this point in my life I had no interest in a network marketing business. I just didn't trust them to be legitimate.

We watched a video that told how coffee is the second largest traded commodity in the world. I was blown away. I knew oil was number one, but coffee number two —wow! This coffee is infused with an organic herb that has been used in China for thousands of years. I know that 90 percent of my friends drink coffee. Holding on to my oxygen tank, I turned to Sharon and said, *"We can do this."* We needed an income and this seemed like a great way to get it. We prayed and God answered.

Hope with action and faith does work. We started sharing the coffee and built a good income as a result. Financial needs were met. Then came the real miracle, one that we never expected. Twenty-one days after we started drinking the coffee I put my oxygen tank behind the sofa and haven't used it since. That magical day was September 15, 2013. The following month I visited my physician to have a pulmonary function test (PFT) performed. The PFT test was required every six months for years. The previous one indicated my lungs were functioning at 23 percent of working capacity. Things were different this time. Karen, the PFT tech was amazed and perplexed by the results and had me re-take the test three times that day. She had been conducting the tests since 1984, and had never seen anyone have a better reading than before. She told me the pulmonary physician would give me the results.

Three weeks later I met Dr. Williston again in her office. This time she was blown away with the results. She met me in the lobby and hardly recognized me. I had lost weight and most importantly I stopped using oxygen bottles. My lungs were now functioning at 29 percent of capacity. Hope exploded inside me that day. Hope is when you live a lifestyle of *"believing is seeing"* and not seeing is believing. God was doing a miracle in me, creating a story for the masses. My thoughts went back to the day that He whispered in my soul, *"Your life will influence a multitude of people."*

Hope continued to guide my life. In six months, I had another PFT and this time my lung function was 34 percent, rising even higher to 40 percent at the next six-month test. The test results were highest functioning level I had achieved in 13 years. By now a lot of my friends and even strangers were beginning to ask what I was doing. You see, until now no one had ever reversed COPD (chronic obstructive pulmonary disease). *"How did you do this? How did you get better? This is amazing. This is a miracle."* We heard those statements often.

God's word says, *"I assure you that if you have faith the size of a mustard seed, you could say to this mountain, 'Go from here to there,' and it will go. There will be nothing that you can't do."* (Matthew 17:20) I believe this is true. However, when the mountain is gone we must do our part. We need to stand up, leave our comfortable chair and travel to the other side where the mountain was located. It is not going to come to us. We need to venture out and retrieve it. Quite simply, faith must have works.

This is when I realized that God blessed me with healthier lungs so I could do everything in my ability to become the best I could be. God was telling me, *"You have your miracle, what are you going to do with it?"* I needed to get more serious about my health, which means completely changing my way of thinking and making healthy food choices. This body we have is God's temple and we need to keep it clean. Proper eating, thinking and speaking must become the guideposts for our lives. These contribute to our overall wellness — body, mind and soul. Because God has been so good to me I feel the need to become the best I can be. I started walking two to five miles a day and went on a serious healthy living program. Up to this point I have lost 125 pounds and continue to work hard at becoming better.

By the time you read this I will be a published author as well as an international speaker. I have told my story to more than 18,000 people in over fifty countries. My daily routine now is to pour value into as many people as possible. God is good and faithful to those who focus on His purpose for their lives, and not on our purpose.

My desire is that everyone who reads my story of HOPE will make a decision to follow my footsteps and trust in God and his mercy. Become all you can be for His purpose for you.

#copdwarrior @wendellbettscopdwarrior

"My Grace is sufficient for you. For power is perfected in weakness. Most gladly I will rather boast of my weaknesses so that the power of Christ may dwell in me."
Second Corinthians 12:9

"But I have trusted in your loving kindness. My heart shall rejoice in your salvation. I will sing to the Lord because he has dealt with me bountifully."
Psalms 13:5-6

"For I know the plans I have for you…. Plans to give you hope and a future."
Jeremiah 29:11

STRATEGIES FOR IGNITING YOUR FIRE OF HOPE

1. Hope! What is Hope?

_____

_____

_____

_____

2. Where does hope come from?

_____

_____

_____

_____

3. How do we keep our Hope?

_____

_____

_____

_____

4. Is Hope real? Is it reasonable to believe in and have Hope?

_____

_____

_____

_____

ABOUT WENDELL BETTS

Wendell Betts is a Best Selling Author as well as an International speaker and Certified John Maxwell team member. Wendell is a Life Coach as well as a Leadership teacher and Mentor.

Wendell grew up in a small farming community in Eastern Canada with big dreams. His mother taught him that nothing was impossible and that he could do or be anything he wanted or had a desire to be. Wendell learned how to milk cows at the age of 5 and operate a farm tractor by the age of 8. Wendell was always a dreamer and his dreams were always larger than life. By the age of 48 Wendell owned 18 tractor trailers and had done very well for himself.

Wendell's life has changed due to a horrific disease but through that he even stayed positive and refused to quit. His story is miraculous and one that needs to be heard throughout the universe. His mission now is to pour value into as many people as possible and to leave a legacy of Hope and Faith.

Contact Wendell:

- Website: www.CLPLI.com/Wendell_Betts
- Facebook: www.Facebook.com/Wendell.Betts.9
- Email: wdbetts53@msn.com
- Email: wdsebetts@gmail.com
- Phone: 506-454-8689
- Cell Phone: 506-897-1786 (texting only please)

THE GIFT OF HOPE

By Laura Campbell

THE GIFT OF HOPE

When I graduated from high school, life took a turn. My parents were going through a tough divorce. My father was seeing another woman. My world was turned upside down. I grew up in a close, Italian family where we shared most Sunday afternoons and holidays at my grandparents, on my father's side, sharing great food and fun times. What would this mean? How could my father do something like this to us? What would happen to my mother, who only worked part time for a friend? What about my three younger siblings? I was in disbelief at first, but became angry. The thoughts of my father being so strict with me, while being unfaithful to my mother brewed in my mind. His voice echoed, *"You don't need college. You're only going to get married and be a mother anyway."* I knew from that moment, that I would find a way to go to college and never depend on anyone to support me. It would become my goal, my hope. We didn't see my father much after he left, and sadly saw his family less as well.

From the time we were little, my mother took us to church every week, but not always the same one. Most of the time masses were in English, although sometimes they were in Italian and other times in Polish, but we were told that God is listening, so pray anyway. I don't think my mother knew the faith she was instilling in me at the time, but it was that faith that built my hope. I learned how to pray. I will never forget walking into church on a Monday evening after my father left, and I saw a group of older women in black veils chanting Novena prayers in Italian. It felt uncomfortable at first, but then I remembered that God listens in all languages. I believe this is where my hope began to seed. I felt heard and comforted in church. It was the place where I turned in times of difficulty. Most 18 year olds may have gone other places, but this is where hope and faith first met for me.

I needed to find a job after graduation. After several interviews, I was given an entry level position at a local bank. I learned every role within the branch office and felt valuable. I enjoyed helping my mom financially and paying the small mortgage she was left with. I fostered connections with our customers and was awarded a few promotions. After helping my mother get back on her feet, and better than ever, she was offered employment at a foster care Agency. I decided to give my notice and finally go to college!

My boss was speechless and approved tuition reimbursement if I stayed. The catch was that my degree had to be in finance or banking. I was thrilled at the opportunity and started classes the following week. Finance and banking were never interests I would have chosen, but it was being given to me and was the only foreseeable hope of reaching my goal of supporting myself.

One Friday evening, a client and I were conducting business at my desk. He said he has watched me work so hard and was wondering why I wasn't promoted to a bank officer yet? I gave our conversation some thought and approached my branch manager with this question. He told me that I was only 21 and although I did the work, I was too young. When I told my client, he said, *"That's ridiculous. Are you standing for that?"* I thought about the paid college tuition and steady job, but how would I achieve my goal of being able to support myself well, if I couldn't be promoted further? What age was sufficient to be an officer? He couldn't tell me. I couldn't make agreements with his limiting beliefs.

A few weeks later, I met a good friend at a local pub and we began to catch up on what we were doing. He told me that he was an officer in corporate banking in New York City. He agreed with my client and said he would be happy to get me an interview with his bank. I was scared. Even though I lived on Long Island, I was never in New York City and I wouldn't have a clue how to get around. I imagined the city as a giant, gloomy place, where crime was spiraling and I would always have to be looking over my shoulder. I'm petite and barely 5 feet tall, it seemed overwhelming, but the girl with hope quickly said, *"Yes, I would love that!"* The next morning, I called a friend, who worked in Midtown Manhattan, to tell him the story. He suggested that we meet at the train station and offered to accompany me to the bank. I was so grateful for people willing to help me. There are angels on earth!

The morning of the interview, I had so many limiting beliefs. What would they say when they heard that I didn't complete my four-year degree? What would they think of my age? I didn't have the experience to do this. I knew nothing about the city. Would they even take me seriously? I hushed those thoughts and dressed in my new outfit, grabbed a cup of tea, and met my friend at the train. I was anxious about taking the subway, but had faith that my friend knew the way. The interview was in the private and corporate banking department of a large New York Bank and seemed to go well. Toward the end, a bank employee came in to ask a question about a large transaction for a client. The vice president conducting the interview asked me what I would do. I answered on the spot by drawing on my client relationship skills and it happened to be the answer that he wanted to hear. I was to start a training program in two weeks, but I had to finish my degree while I worked. It all happened so fast!

I couldn't believe how my life was changing and aligning with my goal. I was promoted to a bank officer within a year of completing the training program. My salary increased and I was suddenly able to support myself and give generously to my family and those in need. I grew to love New York City! It wasn't gloomy, it was exciting, fast paced and people seemed assured and assertive. I wasn't robbed nor feared I would be. I never looked over my shoulder, I was too busy looking at the tall, extraordinary buildings, where successful people thrived! I was going to be one of them...That was my hope.

As I became a confident commuter, I met my future husband on the train. He played soccer for the local pub's team and we knew many of the same people. Unlike my girlfriends, I didn't have dreams of getting married. It wasn't something I focused on. Seeing my parent's marriage end abruptly after 20 years, losing part of my family in the divorce, and watching my mom become so distraught just didn't seem to be worth the risk. Meeting Chris changed all of that. There was something about him that gave me hope and the faith that we could spend our lives together happily. We dated for about a year and decided to get engaged. We were married a year later. I felt confident in the decision, after all, I was successful now, which I thought lowered my *"risk"* of being hurt.

I had become an assistant vice president and still had not completed my degree. My job had demanding hours and it was difficult to make evening classes. Since my team met our quota of new accounts and my clients exhibited their gratitude by referring other high net worth individuals, I continued to be promoted. Chris and I were financially in a great place, we bought a house and talked about a family, but I was hesitant. I knew that would be a big step for me. Bringing children into our marriage made me feel uncertain. I would never want a child to experience what my siblings and I went through. We all carried wounds, even in adulthood. It took time for me to build enough faith in our marriage to have the hope that I needed. I began to see the connection between faith and hope. Faith is trust, assurance and confidence in what we cannot see, which may be affected from past experiences and hope is the anticipation of the good to come. Faith helps us to be more confident in what we hope for and gives us the ability to know something can be real, even if we can't see it. Risks based on hope alone are more difficult to take. It was five years later when our beautiful, healthy baby girl arrived.

I interviewed nannies for a while and extended my maternity leave several times. My boss became concerned that I may resign and gave me the incentive of returning as a vice president. I couldn't imagine how I would go back to work and leave our daughter so far away. Our home on Long Island was over an hour away by train and a 20-minute drive to the train station. My Italian family values began to surface. I found something wrong with everyone I interviewed. After months of this, I pulled from my faith and gave my notice at work. I left my position and life goal of supporting myself. I took the risk and focused on a new hope. The hope of being a mother to the miracle God gave us. My life took another turn.

Not long after I gave notice, I began to second guess myself. I worked so hard to become a high-ranking bank officer, how could I throw it all away? What if my marriage didn't work out? How would my life change without the money? What would I tell people when they asked what I did for a living? My mother became a frequent visitor and used many saved up vacation days to spend time with her granddaughter. When she was visiting one day, I shared some of my feelings with her. She immediately offered to quit her job and stay with Nicole for the salary I would have paid a nanny. My mother finally had a great job, with benefits, a pension and new friends. I was so proud of her. I could never allow her to give that up. Again, the link between faith and hope revealed itself. I had to rely on my faith and I wondered if what I hoped for aligned with God's plan for me. Banking was never my choice, was it meant to be temporary? What if it wasn't my purpose? On my faith, I let go of all I thought I wanted and prayed that God would continue to guide me. I learned that hope is a state of mind and can grow within. I surrendered to my new hope, with the faith of knowing that God would guide me in direction of his plan. It felt reassuring to know that I can develop hope, even when things change or get difficult.

We went on to have two sons. I loved every second of being a mother, even the tough ones. I lived in gratitude. My marriage was unlike any I had witnessed growing up. My hard working husband had great respect and love for me and our family. That gave me faith. I was class mother, religion teacher and I chaired fundraisers at church and at my children's school. I volunteered and helped many in need. I learned the difference between success and significance. Many of my children's friends began to confide in me. When the time came for me to go back to work, I realized that I didn't want to go back to banking. I had a new level of awareness and I truly desired significance.

I went back to college at age 40, starting all over with a different degree. This one was **MY** choice. I wasn't sure what I would do, but had full faith that I would be guided to the place God planned for me all along. I was volunteering as a crisis counselor when I graduated. I sincerely enjoyed working with people who had such a driving dedication and a desire to help those in crisis. The volunteers were selfless and they enriched my hope. One day the associate director presented workshops to students, which was part of our community education program. I mentioned that I would love to do that work. She had faith in me and I became a community educator. They offered me the first available job opening. It was an immediate feeling of being exactly where I belonged.

As a crisis counselor, I constantly find myself in situations where I give hope to others. I have developed a keen sense of hope. I can find it in the simplest of things, such as a cup of vanilla tea, a sunset, the beach, a candle and a prayer. When people feel hopeless, it helps to explore the little bits of light in their darkness. This can be difficult because the darkness is vast and the lights are just little glimmers. If we chase the glimmers of light, we will find hope. Being an empathetic listener helps us to key in on just where the glimmers are hidden in someone's life.

As I look back, I realize that hope played a pivotal role in my life. It allowed me to overcome and thrive in tough situations. It was the basis for every transition I experienced. Much like faith, we can develop hope, but without faith, hope loses its potency. Below are some thoughts I use to develop hope as a state of mind, so that I can continue to give it to others.

1. Have patience and love for yourself, recognize your strengths. Treat yourself as you would your very best friend. Love produces hope.

2. Life is ever-changing and creating possibilities every day. Let go of attachments, live in the possibilities and have faith in God's plan for you. Practice faith. Surrender to hope.

3. What you focus on expands. Focus on what you have, not what you don't have. Gratitude reminds us of hope.

4. Be aware of other challenging times when you overcame obstacles and difficulty. Feel the strength that filled you then. Have faith that you can access it again. Hope is inner strength.

5. Dark times are opportunities for finding the glimmers of light. Challenge yourself to look for them. Those are our greatest learning moments. After all, it is only in the darkness that we can see the stars. There is hope in darkness. There is hope everywhere.

Once we can develop hope in our lives, we can recognize it easily in others. Sometimes, giving hope could sound as effortless as, *"Are you okay?"* or *"I'm concerned about you."* Small words that say *"You're not alone"* and *"I care"* convey hope. Even when one thinks about giving up, hearing that someone cares can replenish the hope needed to keep on going.

> *"Now these three remain: faith, hope and love.*
> *But the greatest of these is love."*
> Corinthians 13:13.

The relationship between Faith, Hope and Love was experienced for me recently, as I watched my daughter and her fiancé pledge their love forever. The faith in each other and God, gave them hope of a beautiful life to come. Their joy began with true love for each other, but when it was mixed with faith, immense hope was created for all to see! That is the power of the three most special gifts: **Faith, Hope and Love.**

When I discovered hope as a state of mind and combined it with developed faith, I found the most powerful formula available to guide through even the toughest of obstacles. Faith fuels hope, it gives it power. The best part is that once it is established, we can zone in on bits of hope, even in the simplest of things and we can be the light for someone else. I believe that hope is a gift that is made to give away. We were meant to be the hope and light for one another. Shine on.

STRATEGIES FOR IGNITING YOUR FIRE OF HOPE

1. What thoughts cross your mind daily? Are they hopeful? We become our thoughts…

_____

_____

_____

_____

2. Is your faith strong enough to fuel your hope?

_____

_____

_____

_____

3. Think about some challenges where you combined faith and hope? What difference did it make?

_____

_____

_____

_____

4. How do you give hope to others?

_____

_____

_____

_____

5. Does your goal align with God's purpose for you? Are you willing to find out?

_____

_____

_____

_____

ABOUT LAURA CAMPBELL

Laura Campbell enjoyed a successful career in corporate and private banking, before transitioning into her favorite role of Mother, and then again into a profession as a Crisis Counselor and Community Education Coordinator at a leading crisis center in Long Island, NY. She is passionate about educating and empowering people to be aware of their thoughts and live consciously. She enjoys giving the gift of hope.

Laura is a certified John C. Maxwell International Coach, Speaker and Leadership Trainer. She has led many exciting, effective Mastermind Groups and feels honored to act as a thinking partner with her Coaching Clients, who are reaching their highest potential.

Laura is the founder of *Infinity Growth and Development*, which brings together Leadership and Mental Health Awareness. She practices personal growth and development daily and believes that our mental health is reflected in how we lead our lives. John Maxwell says, *"The toughest person to lead is always yourself."* Laura believes that we are not our circumstances and that facts can be changed. She has changed her facts many times and is living a life of significance, empowerment and mindfulness. She welcomes you to join her!

Contact Laura:

- Website: www.InfinityGrowthAndDevelopment.com
- Website: www.JohnMaxwellGroup.com/LauraCampbell
- Facebook: www.Facebook.com/profile.php?id=1644067120
- Email: Laura@InfinityGrowthAndDevelopment.com
- Phone: 516-768-8343

THE INTENSITIES OF HOPE

By Jacquie Fazekas

THE INTENSITIES OF HOPE

Hope is like hot sauce! It adds flavor, but to varying degrees based on the intensity selected! Mild to super hot, the ingredients and amount added guides the flavor and intensity.

Hope is the secret sauce, adding both a powerful feeling and belief. However, in each of us, there are varying intensities of hope dependent on the level of ingredients added - **commitment, trust, respect, faith and love**. The level of intensity dictates the power of hope.

The lowest level of intensity is when a person believes and hopes in an outcome or result without any personal action, accountability or pain. I call this level *"Lazy Hope."* It is passive, making it easy to deflect blame to others when hopes fail to become reality. With a low personal investment in the feeling or belief, there is a less positive impact. As well, when hope is centered on self and not serving, it has a low impact result.

I can reflect on many moments that I hoped for results, but failed to put personal action in play. I didn't hold myself to accountable, or experience any pain. Hoping for weight loss in my early years was one of those moments. I listened to what I should do, but I was inconsistent in my actions and commitment to the endeavor. With every feeling of pain or need to sacrifice food choices, I would quickly quit. I had hope, but it really added very little flavor to my life and I got none of the expected results.

The second level of intensity is when one believes and feels that hope is possible if they try hard and persevere through pain. It is a lower level of intensity because it is based on a self-centered belief system that the person alone is responsible for the outcome and result. There is little faith, trust, commitment, love and respect for others in the process and certainly little trust in God. I call this *"Ego-Centered Hope."* When I was in my twenties, and hoped for career advancement, I thought if I worked hard, sacrificed exercising and taking care of myself, and focused solely on my career, the promotions would come. I sacrificed spending quality time with my kids. When I was with them, I was not truly present. Multi-tasking was a way I convinced myself I was in control. In retrospect, it was just a lie I told myself to help from spiraling out of control. In reality, I was desperately out of control. I thought I knew what was best for me and certainly trusted myself more than others. I was only committed to myself, even though I had told myself otherwise. Unconsciously, I told myself everyone around me was there to serve my ego and my goals. I was not serving them. I continued to hope for those promotions. Some came and some went. Over the years, my life and self-awareness continued to grow through various painful moments. Low level hope got me part of the way there, but certainly not at the intensity that I had wished.

The third level of hope's intensity is fairly average. I call it the *"World View of Hope."* In this scenario, the person remains very much self-centered, trying to control the outcome with hope driven feelings and beliefs, periodically reaching out to God for guidance along the way. Often, during the toughest times, those with the *"World View of Hope"* will reach out to others. The shift in reliance to others is important because it awakens the power and intensity of hope. God and others begin to answer requests, rally positive energy and fulfill hopes! For many, hopes and dreams can only be fulfilled with community based support. The term, *"It takes a Village,"* is accurate. It takes more than one person to make things happen in life. Those who hold onto a strong ego-centered view only attracts weakness.

In my thirties, I started to shift to the *"World View."* A few years after the birth of my second son, I found myself in a crumbling marriage that had once had been strong. The years prior were full of self-centered activities and choices that had eventually eroded my relationships. I speak of my relationships to my husband, my children, my extended family and friends, but most importantly myself! The weeks and months after my divorce soon propelled me into a greater self-awareness. As I was growing in self-awareness and enduring significant pain, I boldly expressed my commitment to serving my children, making them the number one priority in my life above all else. I told my mother and others that I met, I would sacrifice everything that I had accomplished in my life and give up my job if necessary, in order to serve and support my boys. The addition of all those needed ingredients, commitment, trust, respect, faith and love intensified my hope. I called out to God to help me! I finally had learned I could not raise my children on my own. No matter what will power, pain or perseverance I had, my human **Will** was not enough. It was at this time in my life, I called out for help, trusting and respecting others. I committed to others and had faith beyond myself. From that moment, my *"Village"* was provided to me! I never knew how I was going to do it, but I had hope! Voila, a more intense hope than before, which resulted in many miracles.

One time I was scheduled to travel overseas on a two-week work trip. At the last minute, I discovered that my ex-husband would not take the boys while I traveled. Now, with no one to take care of my kids, God answered with a miracle. I was sobbing uncontrollably one day, while picking my boys up at the Montessori school. Amanda, their pre-school teacher, came to my support without me even asking. She stepped up and said, *"I'll watch the boys!"* For many years later, Amanda watched the boys while I traveled. From that experience, I began to believe in the power of feeling hopeful! With the right ingredients, the intensity of hope can move mountains in your life. Since then, I have had a Village come to my rescue to help serve and support me as a single working mom!

The fourth level of intensity revolves around serving others. When hope is focused on positive belief and feelings for others, the intensity is heightened. Positive energy propels positive outcomes. God and others recognize the level of selflessness in the vision, goals and desires. When a person reaches out in faith to God, requesting support, and acknowledging personal limitations, God listens intently. A strong commitment to personal sacrifice to support positive outcomes further serves as evidence to all that it is worthy of hope to be fulfilled. I call this level of hope *"Selfless-Positive Hope."* For much of my adult life, I maintained a third level *"worldly view"* of hope. Intense and rewarding, but not as intense as it could be to achieve results. Only in my late forties have I come to realize that the ingredients I put into my hopeful life determines the final outcome. The biggest shift came when I truly relinquished control of the hopes and dreams I have for my boys to God. Up to the moment they left for college, I was holding on to a subtle belief that I could help control the outcome of their lives. I suspect I was not much different from most hopeful parents, only wanting the best for our children. I thought I knew what was best for them and hoped no harm would come to them while they were out of sight at college. Really! My prayers were weak until I realized I needed to start believing in God's **Will** to be done, not mine. Yes, a false weak hope soon turned to an intense hope relying on God as the ultimate guide of their lives and mine. I started to use my time, energy and focus toward serving others and not myself or my boys. I stopped worrying about my boys, trusting that they would be taken care and hopeful for them that they encounter growth, pain, sacrifice and all the various blessings that comes with God's oversight and vision for them. Soon blessings flowed to them! The power of greater intense hope!

The fifth and final level of intensity is rooted in an unwavering belief and feeling of commitment, trust, faith, respect and love for the process of self-love, selflessness and self-sacrifice. This hope is for fulfillment of one's unique purpose on earth. By learning to love, listen, honor and follow our individual spirit, we have courage to recognize the calling to serve in our unique way, activating an energy that vibrates throughout the Universe! This intensity of hope is vibrated throughout the entire universe and resources and results happen! This I call the *"Abundant Hope."* It is the unwavering focus to be fulfilled through self-love and self-sacrifice. Unwavering commitment, trust, faith, respect, and love for the process and endurance of pain allows each of us to dial into the degree of hope that renders most people speechless. It is the very intense degree of hope that becomes the fuel to propel us into great acts of courage and selfless acts of kindness. Our true purpose is often revealed during this time. It serves to create what we see and call miracles today! Small or large miracles as a result of having the most intense hope! For me, self-love was the last ingredient to be added. Through lovingly serving others, like family, friends, coworkers, and with my volunteer work, I started to experience powerful results from my hopeful heart. I would pray for others and serve others. However, I recently realized that no matter what level of service I was giving, if I was not serving and loving myself, I could not truly, intensely serve others or fulfill my purpose on earth. For forty years, I had asked God to reveal my purpose on earth, but despite my hopes for the answer, it was never revealed to me fully until I learned to love myself. The hope for my purpose to be revealed began to intensify as my awareness of my spirit began. With every revelation came a moment to love, appreciate and listen to my spirit. The power of purpose is the most intense when you are truly listening to the calling of your soul!

For the soul only wants to serve others and fulfill the calling from God! The universe summons support and serves the intensely hopeful heart! It has taken hours of reflection and of prayer for me to understand the Intensities of Hope in my own life.

We are each born with a purpose. We have passions that stir in us, but are never called on to be used. So often, we allow the comforts of our current existence to numb us into sleepy living. We rely on low levels of hope to push us to the next level, but are quick to blame the outside world for hope not being answered. Many live in a defeated mindset and never wake to fight and live a purpose driven life. However, sometimes our spirit is so restless it creates tension and pain to shake us awake. If you are reading this and feel the rumblings in your belly, wake up! It is time to be brave and start loving yourself unconditionally and others so you can seek out your purpose. Start living your life serving others and spice up your life with the intense flavors of, commitment, trust, respect, faith and love. Turning up the heat and intensity of your hope will reveal your true purpose. Do not waste days and years asleep. Let your Spirit free! I challenge you to participate in quiet reflection each day with God, authentically asking to be relinquished of selfish, judgmental and ego-based thoughts. With an authentic heart and loving intentions, hope begins to flow and awaken a dormant spirit. With a stimulated excited **spirit, joy, love and selflessness** begin to take hold and propels and intense hope that tingles all your sense. The power of hope calls on all to serve you and support your purpose. It is amazing with every moment, when your eyes are wide open, you see miracles laid in front of you ushering you toward a selfish impactful life. This is called living significantly.

It is with the unwavering intensity of hope and passion toward your authentic purpose that you reach your greatest fulfillment.

I lovingly hope that you are inspired to reflect on your own level of hope and seek ways to intensify your hope so you can truly live out your purpose. Your greatest calling and authentic purpose is awaiting you!

STRATEGIES FOR IGNITING YOUR FIRE OF HOPE

1. In reflection, where are you in your intensity of hope?

_____

_____

_____

_____

2. Do you have stirring in your belly that you are meant to do more with your life?

_____

_____

_____

_____

3. What is holding you back from turning up the heat on your life?

_____

_____

_____

_____

4. What vision do you have for your life?

_____

_____

_____

_____

5. What daily shifts can you make in your thoughts and prayers that will spice things up?

_____

_____

_____

_____

ABOUT JACQUIE FAZEKAS

Jacquie Fazekas has a passion for helping others find their purpose and passion. Throughout her struggles, she has always possessed a positive and resilient attitude. Jacquie lives her life passionately every day, encouraging others to live positively too. Jacquie understands the power of overcoming failure and fears.

Jacquie was born in Canada and moved to Naples, Florida when she was 13 years old. Since then, she has lived in many cities throughout the USA and traveled globally. Everyone in the world struggles and each person has their unique lessons to learn. With her passion to serve others, she is seeking out other ways to serve more people in a greater capacity. Passionate about holistic health and wellness, she shares her illness experiences with others in hope of sparking more awareness about the importance of living a holistic healthy lifestyle. Today, she is an active hospice volunteer and mentors many young professionals she has touched over the years. As a Certified John C. Maxwell International Coach, Speaker and Trainer, she seeks to continue to serve others in their growth journey, meeting them where they are today and encouraging them along their way.

Contact Jacquie:

- Website: www.JohnMaxwellGroup.com/JacquieFazekas
- Facebook: www.Facebook.com/JacquieFazekas
- LinkedIn: www.LinkedIn.com/in/Jacquie-Fazekas
- Email: JRFazekas@gmail.com
- Phone: 479-366-2838

HOPE FOUND IN THE HAND OF GOD

By Marilee Harrington

HOPE FOUND IN THE HAND OF GOD

As I walked into the classroom to begin my four-month student internship, I was a shy and insecure 22-year-old. However, I was so blessed to have an amazing, supportive teacher who guided me in the right direction. She took me aside one day and asked, *"What is holding you back?"* She was right, there was something holding me back.

"I wasn't a great student in school. I didn't have great marks," I answered quietly. I can still hear her voice and have never forgotten her words. *"Good students don't always make good teachers,"* she replied. At that moment, I was empowered and my hope of being a teacher was renewed. I knew I could be a good teacher, maybe even a great teacher.

Teaching is all I've ever wanted to do. At the age of six I decided to be a teacher, and kept my eye on the goal. Being shy would make it difficult, but I knew God had plans for me. However, school was challenging and I was always sick. How was I ever going to strive to be what I believed God wanted me to be? Many times, I cried out to God asking for healing, but it never came. Although it was difficult, I kept my faith and hope that God had an amazing plan for my life. I continued to pray for relief and the possibility of healing, which I sort of knew would never come. Not because I didn't think God could do it, but I believed He had a purpose for it.

When I was in my early teens, Dad called me and my siblings into the living room. He said his minister's salary wasn't abundant enough to pay our college tuition, and each of us children should start saving to pay for that expense. Next in what can only be described as a fatherly blessing, Dad spoke to us individually. First came my eldest sister. She was a good student and he recommended that she pursue a career in medicine. To my older, and only brother, he suggested a career in business. My younger sister was destined to become a nurse, based on Dad's wisdom. Finally, it was my turn, and I was excited to hear my father's suggestion for me. He said, *"Marilee, I don't think university is for you. But don't worry, we'll take care of you."*

WHAT? I know he meant it as a loving gesture, but that wasn't going to happen.

I stood straight up, and declared, *"I'm going to be a teacher, and that's that!"*

As I stormed out of the room I could hear my father's voice trailing after me, *"Then become a teacher."*

As I entered high school, it soon became evident that I couldn't keep up with all the material and make the necessary marks to attend university. By grade 12, I watched as my dream slipped between my fingers. Crying out to God I asked, *"What was it all for?"* I had been a good girl. I had trusted him and shared my faith. I had tried hard to succeed in high school, and now the one thing I had ever known He wanted me to do was slipping away.

One day as I walked down a long corridor lined with office doors, I heard my guidance counselor call to me. To this day, I don't know how she even knew my name. I turned and walked back to her, and she said, *"I see you haven't applied to university yet."*

"No", I said sadly. *"My marks are too low, and I'd never be accepted into the education program."*

"Apply anyway," she said, and I nervously submitted my application. The thought of a rejection letter loomed over me, but that is where God stepped in and showed that He had a plan for my life. When the letter arrived it wasn't a rejection, but rather an acceptance. I was classified as a returning student. How could this be? As I continued to read through the letter I was blown away by how God had made it all possible. During the summer before grade 12 my younger sister had convinced me to take a computer course with her at the local university, so I did and I passed. Yes, it was a C, but it was a pass. And that is all the university saw when my application was received.

God had everything under control all the time. There was, and still is, no question in my mind that I only went to university by the grace of God. I spent the next four years in the education program. I started off in the elementary program, only to discover I really didn't enjoy little children. I switched into secondary education with a history major. There I knew I had found my niche. God constantly showed me where and what he wanted me to do. I just had to be willing to follow His path.

After graduation I married a wonderful, Godly man and entered the world of unemployment. I had always worked as a child. Sitting around wasn't in my nature. I decided to start my own business, but it didn't involve teaching and I needed to be doing the work God intended for me. When an opportunity to teach kindergarten arose, I grabbed it, but after a few months I knew this wasn't my final destination. I took the leap of faith and began substitute teaching. Soon God opened the door to my first real teaching position. Sounds awesome, doesn't it? I wish I could say it was. I kindly refer to it as the *"job from hell."* Reality became a daily affirmation that my chosen career, one where honesty, integrity and kindness were supposed to be paramount, was just an illusion. How could some people be so unkind? I remember so many days crying all the way home. Thank goodness, I had nearly two hours to do that. God and I had many conversations and pleas during those hours, but nothing changed. If anything, the situation worsened. *"Why would God send me to such a terrible place?"* I asked. As the years passed I became more ill, but I was determined not to let it destroy me. I knew God had appointed me to be a teacher and I was going to fight.

It was around this time my husband and I were blessed with our first child. We had been told we could never have children, so our baby girl truly was a blessing, especially as my illness worsened. A year later, unexpectedly, our second child arrived, soon followed by a third. By then I had my diagnosis, but it wasn't bone cancer as feared. Instead it was a severe case of fibromyalgia. I would live, but I would be in pain for the rest of my life. And the physicians were right. I have experienced chronic pain at various intensities over the past 26 years, but I'm still breathing! It wasn't until I accepted this as God's way of demonstrating His love and compassion for me that I truly began to understand what I was going through. My pain was His way of keeping me close to Him, because I would always need Him to help me endure it.

After three years in the *"job from hell,"* God reached down and pulled me out of that horrible place, and sent me to the school where I knew He always wanted me to be. If I learned anything from that first job, it was how not to treat people. God taught me a valuable lesson. The new school had been the trophy placement desired by many, but God had fast tracked me there in three years. It was truly a miracle. I finally understood why he had left me in the *"job from hell."* Sometimes we have to walk through the fires of tribulation to reach our destination of purpose.

I soon connected with the school's Youth for Christ program. What an amazing experience it was to work with kids who were eager to share Christ with their peers. The group of eight dedicated youth, escalated to nearly a 100 young people on fire for Christ. Their presence was noticeable in the school.

I remember one Youth for Christ meeting where we watched a video series for youth spiritual growth, *"Life on the Edge,"* by James Dobson. The video that day was particularly powerful and had great meaning for my life. Once again God was telling me not to lose hope. Although my health was not improving, He understood my pain and was suffering with me. When I cried in pain, He was crying with me. With tears in my eyes, God had once again shown me what an amazing and loving God He is.

When everything is moving smoothly and predictably in God's direction, watch for Satan to rev up his attacks. All my life I could sense things that were about to happen, or had dreams where God revealed things to me. He told me in a dream that the youth program would grow to nearly 100 students, and it did. In a later dream, He revealed how that was all about to change. One night I awoke from a heart-wrenching dream in tears. The dream was so real, and heartbreaking. The next day I went to speak with one of the school guidance counselors, who also was a Christian. The dream had become such a burden I needed to speak with someone. She agreed it was from God, and said I had a decision to make. I could address it, or wait for it to happen.

I chose to address it, knowing that it likely wouldn't change the final outcome. The school had established a youth outreach program that was supported by several local pastors. The amazing monthly *"Sunday night live"* services were attracting youth from around the city. I approached the youth pastor who was in my dream and asked that he be respectful of the interdenominational make-up of the YFC group. A more conservative congregation was scheduled to host the next *"Sunday night live"* service. My heart broke when I got word that my dream had come true and he had offended a number of people. *"Why?"* I asked God. It was from this point the once vibrant group began to wane. Satan had used a Christian to do his work.

God was not done yet, as he began to redirect my attention in new ways. It was time to go, but I didn't want to go. After a year of fighting with God, and feeling like Jonah, I finally obeyed Him and jumped ship, transferring to the second local high school. Here my mission for Christ changed. I thought for sure it was to continue working with Youth for Christ, but instead it was more of a one-on-one sharing of Christ. Sunday school kids and others came to talk about God. My lunch hours were once again time with Christ, but in a different way. When my workload was always at its height, God would send someone to ask a question or ask for prayer. I learned early in my career that work can always be done later, but someone needing prayer was urgent.

Just when you think you've got it all figured out, God puts a twist in the road. Thinking I was going to be teaching Modern History I was informed that I would be teaching Ancient History. *"What???"* How could this happen. I had no background in Ancient History, and I actually avoided it in university because I disliked it so much in high school. I clearly remember walking from my classroom down to the staff room, butting my head on the table and sobbing. *"God, what are you doing?"*

The following September I began teaching the Ancient History course. Needless to say, I complained all the way until near the end of the semester. It was then that God revealed to me through a song that He wanted me to learn Ancient history to understand Him more. For history is *"His Story,"* and now being placed in the context of what was happening in the ancient world I would learn so much more about Him. Tears were shed that day, with the realization that God was trying to draw me closer. Those ancient stories I had learned as a child were brought to life as I plotted them in history and saw how God used His people to influence the ancient world.

I think one of the more tangible experiences I had, which confirmed in my heart that God wanted me to be a teacher and He was always by my side, was the year I lost a student to a house fire. The student, a girl, had been a part of a particularly challenging class. Basically, the students were just mean kids. They were mean to me, to their peers and even to themselves. It took everything I had to teach that class every day. A few days after my student died the class was taking a test. As usual I stood at the back of the class praying over them, and for myself. *"God, I don't think I can do this much longer. It's just too hard."* Suddenly I felt a hand of comfort rest on my shoulder. Yes, it startled me, and when I turned to see who it was, there was only the filing cabinet behind me. Joy filled my heart with the real understanding that I wasn't in this alone. God was with me every step of the way and I didn't need to fear. It is moments like that I'm humbled and reminded that I am a teacher only by the love and grace of God. His purpose is for me to be there and be a beacon of light for Him.

My growth and challenges as a teacher spilled over into my home life, and the skills God taught me were used there too. God had made me a fighter for the weak, even when I was weak. By the time my children entered school, I became their champion, their voice for the right to learn. God had set me aside from the responsibilities of Youth for Christ to give me time to nurture and fight for my own children. Our eldest is hearing impaired. She had been told by the public-school system she would never succeed. But God is bigger than them and she now holds two university degrees and is on her own unique and special journey with God. Our middle child was reading at a grade 2 level in grade 5. God reached down into his heart and gave him the desire to try and do it alone. He went on to complete a degree in engineering. Our third child was told he would never learn to read or write. I said he would. With a lot of prayer and work he was successful, and now as an adult he is working on his Masters in engineering.

How is it possible that teachers had given up on all three, in the very same profession that I believed would help them? I thought we were supposed to fight for kids to succeed, to encourage them to reach higher than even they thought possible. Teachers are there to comfort students when they fall, and help them stand again. However, where the public school failed my children, the local Christian school nurtured success. I'm not saying Christian schools are made up of perfect people because we are all human, but the school my children attended was filled with God-fearing teachers and administrators who loved the Lord. They truly loved and prayed for my children. As time passed I saw how God used the faculty to help shape and mold my children into Godly youth. The values and truths I was teaching at home were being upheld and supported at school. Thank you, God, for making public school such a detestable place for my children.

By the time my children entered the university God began a new direction for our family. Two weeks before a new school year began, my sister asked if we knew anyone who could take a foreign student for the year. The housing arrangement had fallen through and the student would be arriving in two weeks. I knew in my gut this was the next phase for our lives. My husband and I had discussed the possibility years earlier and I knew now was the time. What originally was taking care of one international student soon became several young people. We desired to be a blessing to these young people, but in reality, they became a blessing to us as well.

Today we are engaged in full time mission work, caring for international students in Christian school housing. And yes, we are both working full time too. My friends think I'm crazy, unable to accept the idea of an empty nest. But the truth is, it has been an answer to prayer. Way back when I was diagnosed with fibromyalgia, the doctor told me that if I wanted to keep walking, my job and kids would help. They would give me purpose to move each day. Now with retirement looming and my kids grown, I was beginning to fear I would have no reason to keep putting one foot in front of the other. God has proved once again that he is in control and that he still has a lot of other things He needs me to do. Each morning when I rise, I thank God for another day that I can walk. So, I shall continue to walk with him, for He has never failed me. For the one truth, I have held true since I was in high school is in Proverbs 3:6, *"In all your ways acknowledge Him and He will direct your path."* And that He has done. He has given me hope when there seemed to be none, and shown me the path to take. It may not always be easy, or the one I'd like to travel, but it'll be the perfect one laid out by a perfect God. Isaiah 55:9 says, *"For as the heavens are higher than the earth, so are my ways higher than your ways and my thoughts than your thoughts."*

I was once asked if I regretted all the hardships and challenges in my life. My answer is wholeheartedly, no. My life journey has given me hope and faith beyond what I would otherwise have known. I have a relationship with God that I could never give up, and I long for it to grow even stronger. My journey has taught me that my strength and hope comes from Him.

STRATEGIES FOR IGNITING YOUR FIRE OF HOPE

1. When life is full of challenges, how do we react to them? Do you find hope in what seems hopeless? Why or why not?

_____

_____

_____

_____

2. Do you feel that God is leading you to accomplish something for him, but are afraid of failing at it? If our hopes and desires are founded in Christ, then he will direct your path. Go with His leading and he will open and shut doors as He directs your life.

_____

_____

_____

_____

3. Read Isaiah 30:18. (Amplified, classic Edition) *"And therefore the Lord [earnestly] waits [expecting, looking, and longing] to be gracious to you; and therefore, He lifts Himself up, that He may have mercy on you and show loving-kindness to you. For the Lord is a God of justice. Blessed (happy, fortunate, to be envied) are all those who [earnestly] wait for Him, who expect and look and long for Him [for His victory, His favor, His love, His peace, His joy, and His matchless, unbroken companionship]!"*

Now, how do you feel about the dreams and desires of your heart? Are you ready to step out in faith?

_____

_____

_____

_____

ABOUT MARILEE HARRINGTON

 Born in northern Manitoba, Canada, Marilee moved several times in her youth, until settling down in Douglas, New Brunswick. There she and her loving, supportive husband raised three active children, while pursuing her career as a teacher. Although faced with numerous challenges and blessings, Marilee has managed to stand fast in her faith, giving hope and encouragement to others as God leads her. With God's strength, she has maintained a fairly active life, including participating in her local church and with the local Christian school's International Homestay program.

As an educator, Marilee teaches most effectively through story telling. Thus, writing feels like a natural transition as she nears the end of a 30-year teaching career. Marilee is delighted to write about her life experiences, with the hope of inspiring others.

Contact Marilee

- Email: Harringtonmdrw@gmail.com

A FATHER'S LOVE

By Jennifer Johnson

A FATHER'S LOVE

I will always be *"Daddy's little girl."* Chronological age simply doesn't matter. One of my fondest memories of my father is the weekly calls that we enjoyed as I drove home after teaching my class at the college. The father-daughter ritual was a cherished opportunity to discuss world issues, share advice and connect virtually since our schedules rarely allowed for personal visits.

In August 2012, I was leading a faculty in-service when the message came that my father had suffered a stroke and was in intensive care. I was devastated. My *"steady rock"* and *"sounding board"* was struggling and I felt helpless and hopeless. What could I do? Would he be okay? How badly was he affected? Little did I know that this would be the start of a lengthy illness and ultimate death that tested family, faith and friendships.

As my father's health moved up and down like a roller-coaster over the next fifteen months, my mom, sisters and I discovered ways to help father with his daily needs. Each one of us had our own strengths and abilities. Thankfully, my parents lived close by, allowing for more frequent visits and giving me the opportunity to provide assistance whenever possible. My *"value add"* was sitting with my father during his weekly dialysis treatments and being a lunch companion. This allowed us to continue our *"talks,"* and nurture the important father-daughter bond. However, as time went on, difficult decisions had to be made. In November 2013, my father died.

Countless others have lost a parent or loved one and for some, the experience creates a chasm within the family unit, while others have pulled together and become stronger. While each situation may be unique, what I learned through the loss of my own father and how our family navigated the final months of his life has changed and re-defined what hope means to me.

Hope is often defined as *"a feeling of expectation and desire for a certain thing to happen"* or *"to want something to happen or be the case."* People often interchange *"wish"* for *"hope."* A wish is defined as *"something unattainable, with no basis in reality."* When we wish for something, this can often lead to frustration and depression. Hope, on the other hand, connects our faith with a *"real expectation."*

This kind of hope presents itself through our character and endurance.

Character is who we are and presents itself through our behaviors, attitudes and interactions with the world. Endurance is our ability to step forward in the face of adversity despite the physical or emotional affects the situation may have on us.

As we learn in Romans 5:2-5 *"Through him we have also obtained access by faith into this grace in which we stand, and we rejoice in hope of the glory of God. More than that, we rejoice in our sufferings, know that suffering produces endurance, and endurance produces character, and character produces hope, and hope does not put us to shame, because God's love has been poured into our hearts through the Holy Spirit who has been given to us."* As we learn in Romans, to have hope is to have faith in our Heavenly Father. Hope without faith is merely *"wishful thinking."*

Another way to describe character is through values. How we define our values and live them through behaviors helps us to define our purpose or *"why."* Values are developed numerous ways including through culture, family, faith, friends, teachers and life experiences. The values one is raised with may also change as life progresses, or it is possible the value may not change, but the definition, behavior and attitude around the value is altered. The experience of my father's final months brought different meaning to faith, family and friendships and redefined our values and our behaviors tied to those values. This could not have been accomplished without God's grace and his loving message of hope in faith.

Hope...what does it mean and how does one achieve it? How do we lose it? How do we get it back once lost?

The <u>first lesson</u> I learned is to begin by defining our why? We start by identifying what we truly value.

Know your WHY! To know your why is to understand what you value.

In the Hymn written by Joseph Hoskins we read in verse one, *"Though thoughtless thousands choose – the road that leads the soul away from God, this happiness dear Lord be mine. To live and die entirely thine."* A key value that my parents demonstrated throughout their lives, and especially at this difficult time, was their unwavering love and devotion to the Heavenly Father. This value was demonstrated just as we learn in John 3:16 *"For God so loved the world, that he gave his only Son, that whoever believes in him shall not perish but have eternal life."* Their decisions were made through faith, knowing their *"hope"* was eternal life. We rejoice in life, rather than in death, as life through God is eternal. My father may have left this physical earth, yet his love, values, lessons and guidance live on through each one of us who was blessed to be touched by his care and abundance. Father lived out his values authentically. He was a hardworking, caring man, who helped others. His clear demonstration of these values guided my decisions when I chose my soulmate and husband. I searched for the same positive values and strength that my father demonstrated throughout his life. Having a spouse who shares these common values is the firm foundation for a healthy and supportive marriage, much like Christ is the cornerstone of the church's foundation.

The <u>second lesson</u> I learned about achieving hope is to understand how we live out our values. Our behaviors demonstrate what that value looks like. Our behaviors form our character. What does that look like in action and are they congruent?

Define your true values and live them! Once defined, do you live your values each and every day or do you bring them out when it is convenient for you? When it comes to living our values, we have a choice...to live a Godly life true to our authentic values or to live a life of bitterness and anger based on the situation. What do you genuinely value and how can you demonstrate that to the world around you? The value of Family became rooted within us as my father's health declined, yet each one of my siblings, my mother and I demonstrated that value very differently. We were not *"right"* or *"wrong"* in our demonstration of this value, rather it was very personal to each one of us and we supported each other in how we carried that out. This is just one example of the many values we embedded within our core.

> *"but those who hope in the LORD will renew their strength.*
> *They will soar on wings like eagles; they will run and not grow weary,*
> *they will walk and not be faint."*
> Isaiah 40:31

The <u>third lesson</u> to living a hope-filled life is to select an inner circle who SUPPORTS, INSPIRES and GROWS you.

Find your *"Posse"* and grow in their strength. Is your *"Posse"* a source of inspiration and growth? If the person is energy-sucking, it may mean removing them from your inner circle of influence.

As I personally navigated the challenges of my father's situation, I turned to my select inner circle I had assembled over time – some family, some close friends – and this circle had been modified over time. Have you ever had those few close friends who were there by your side, no matter the time of the day or night, making sure that your basic needs are met, insuring that you are taking care of you so that you are able to take care of others? A strong example is the spouse who comforts you and encourages you to remain the strong person that you are, believing in you through better or worse. Other sources of strength can be found in parents, siblings and extended family who support each other and offer words of encouragement and support, reminding us to *"finally, be strong in the Lord and in his mighty power."* Ephesians 6:10.

The <u>fourth lesson</u> to achieving hope is that we may not always understand why or the timing of the end goal, yet what we do know is that God has a plan...

As my father was given one adverse health situation after another, nearly dying multiple times, we (my mother, family, friends and I) could have chosen anger and bitterness. Yet, as much as we were hurting for my father and all that he was going through, we knew that we could rely on the strength of the Lord to guide us through it. My father's passing happened when it was his time to be called home, not when we were ready, but on God's timetable.

> *"For everything there is a season, and a time for every matter under heaven;*
> *a time to be born, and a time to die; a time to plant, and a time to pluck up*
> *what is planted; a time to kill, and a time to heal; a time to break down,*
> *and a time to build up; a time to weep and a time to laugh; a time to mourn,*
> *and a time to dance; a time to cast away stones, and a time to gather stones together;*
> *a time to embrace, and a time to refrain from embracing;..."*
> Ecclesiastes 3:1-22

The <u>fifth and final lesson</u> I have learned is that as life brings twists and turns, our values and behaviors may change, yet we often continue down the same road we started on. Are you truly where you belong and on the right path or is it time for a course correction?

One lesson I have learned from my parents is to live life to the fullest and make memories with those you love as often as you can. To mirror that value, my husband and I took a recent trip to Door County, Wisconsin. It's a place where we find respite, rejuvenation and the opportunity to make wonderful memories. As we were checking out of our resort, I was reflecting on the experiences of the weekend, and walked out to the front walkway to leave. Suddenly I was greeted by dozens of Monarchs fluttering around my head, blocking my vision for a split second, before I could clearly see the beauty of the flowers before me. It was as if the world was telling me to open my eyes and see again...see through the eyes of a child, ask questions, be inquisitive, rather than accept what you see at face value.

I had walked that path numerous times that weekend, in and out, yet that one time walking out to the next place on the agenda, I was greeted with this epiphany:

Be open to what can be, be open to possibilities. Be positive and inquisitive and you will be drawn to where you need to be!

So, what lesson can we learn from this? When we veer off the path, reexamine your why and make course corrections to realign with your values and behaviors when necessary.

When adversity comes into our lives, we often shift to helplessness and hopelessness. Yet, life does not work on our timing, rather on God's timing, and HE is with you no matter what. As we read in Isaiah 43:2 *"When you pass through the waters, I will be with you; and when you pass through the rivers, they will not sweep over you. When you walk through the fire you will not be burned; the flames will not set you ablaze."* God didn't say that we wouldn't have struggles or challenge within our lives. What HE does bring us through our FAITH, is HOPE.

STRATEGIES FOR IGNITING YOUR FIRE OF HOPE

1. Know your WHY!

What is the essence of your existence and what do you value most? Consider writing a list of the key items that you value.

_____

_____

_____

_____

2. Define your true values and live them!

How we define our values is very personal and each word can have a different meaning to every individual. How do others know that we are living out our values? What does that look like in action?

_____

_____

_____

_____

3. Find your *"Posse"* and grow in their strength. This may mean removing some from your circle of influence.

What are some areas you would like to improve in? Who do you admire that can help you to achieve the growth you seek? How can you begin to surround yourself with these people? Who do you need to remove from your circle of influence?

_____

_____

_____

_____

4. Know that God has a plan.

We read in Romans 12:2 *"Do not be conformed to this world, but be transformed by the renewal of your mind, that by testing you may discern what is the will of God, what is good and acceptable and perfect."* We may not understand the path God is leading us toward, yet with patience that plan will unfold. With an attitude of gratitude, what positive movements are you experiencing in your life? What themes do you see as you journal them?

_____

_____

_____

_____

5. When you veer off the path, reexamine your why and course correct when necessary. Are you living out your values? Have your values changes? If so, how and why?

_____

_____

_____

_____

ABOUT JENNIFER JOHNSON

Jennifer Johnson is currently the Associate Dean for the School of Business Accounting, Real Estate and Office Professional Programs at Waukesha County Technical College (WCTC) and also teaches a management course in the School of Business. Jennifer has been working in higher education since 2011. In addition, Jennifer is a certified Leadership Speaker, Trainer and Coach through the John Maxwell Team, an adjunct faculty/curriculum developer for Wisconsin Lutheran College in the Adult and Graduate Studies Program, and has been an adjunct faculty for Edgewood College in Madison teaching in the Returning Adult Accelerated Degree Program.

Jennifer has a passion for empowering others that developed through a partnership with several other women forming *"Power of Your Journey"* workshops and an annual retreat that has grown over the past few years. Participants leave feeling inspired, grounded and energized. Jennifer is honored to have been invited to participate in the Burn Camp Young Adult Leadership Program as a repeat presenter to grow these young leaders and burn survivors.

Jennifer has a passion for impacting others by helping them to achieve the greatest potential through teaching with compassion, through faith in God and by living out one's values in an authentic way.

Contact Jennifer:

- Website: www.JJohnsonLeadLLC.com
- Facebook: www.Facebook.com/LEAD-LLCConsulting-370332040043079
- Email: JJohnsonLeadLLC@gmail.com
- Phone: 262-894-5305

LOOK INSIDE TO SEE OUTSIDE

By Krista Morrissey

LOOK INSIDE TO SEE OUTSIDE

As a professionally certified life and leader coach, I have the pleasure of watching individuals reflect, discover, awaken, own, grow and achieve, right before my eyes. Their journey introduces or reintroduces individuals to the power of courage, reflection, vulnerability, acknowledgment and a plethora of emotions. No one person is like another. It is unique beauty every time, and it energizes and grows me.

At some point in their journey, individuals say, *"I need to find hope. I have lost the fire in my belly. I don't have hope anymore. I have lost my enthusiasm."* These statements are laced with any number of emotions. Individuals are looking to grab onto something to restore their hope. They cannot see the very thing they need, the igniter of hope. They do not understand **they must look inside to see outside.**

Our soul resides deep within us, at our core. It is the essence of who we are. The soul is comprised of values, beliefs, purpose, gifts, energy and vision. ***A healthy soul is our core and grounding.*** With a healthy soul, we are comfortable with who we are and what we have to offer the world. We are full of gratitude for what we have. A healthy soul allows us to look out at the world with a positive perspective, and to have hope that what is coming will be better than what is currently in existence. We hope that where we are is where we are meant to be, but is not where we will stay.

I believe ***hope is enough but also hope is more.*** With hope, you are confident you are enough, while simultaneously knowing you will become more. You will become a better version of yourself. You believe there is more in you, and more out in the world.

As a coach, few statements rattle me, no topic scares me, and seldom do emotions surprise me. However, a theme is appearing in my coaching and my organization development work, that has my attention, and is tugging on my emotions. It involves loss of ownership. So many have lost who they are. They are starving their soul, their compass, their energy tank. They have become blind to their beauty, and the beauty of the world. They have lost hope.

First and foremost, *you belong to you. You own you.* You live according to your own measuring stick. In this space is peace. Peace from understanding self, accepting self and loving self. This space is your fuel. *A healthy soul fuels hope, and hope fuels the soul.* You cannot have one without the other. It starts in the soul.

Most look to others for hope. You cannot take another's hope for your own. You can be energized, inspired or motivated by the hope of others, but you cannot own their hope. You already own hope. Perhaps you need an igniter. Look inside!

Many assume they do not possess what it takes to revitalize their soul. Regularly, clients ask, *"Krista, give me a tool I can use to find... or to be..."* You have everything you need inside of you. Your soul is you. *You own it, so own it.* You have all the components, inside of you, needed to create a healthy soul. Look and listen inside to see outside.

Your soul fuels hope, hope fuels your soul. I believe a healthy soul is comprised of healthy knowledge of four components of you.

Know Who You Are.

I call this **core mining.** Who are you at the core? Miners dig for riches. You must dig for your riches. Your values, beliefs, gifts, purpose, boundaries, energy tank and measuring stick.

Your values are the core of who you are. Values drive behaviors, behaviors create a culture, and you as an individual create a climate inside of a culture. What kind of culture do you create? What kind of climate do you create?

Partnering with values are beliefs, which are based on perspectives gained during life's journey. Values and beliefs are not right or wrong, they belong to each individual. Living outside of either creates angst inside a person. Believing they are universal law creates angst outside of a person.

When the universe creates a person, he or she is given gifts. *What are your gifts?* How will these gifts be used to impact the world? Notice the jewelry that people wear. When shopping (mining) for jewelry, the selection infused the person with happiness, excitement, memories and strength. When one discovers his or her gifts, it is a source of absolute energy, a life guide of what to do with one's time on earth. What saddens me is that we often look at others to view what gifts they have, and wish we had those gifts. Meanwhile, each person's gifts are right there, inside of them, just waiting to be discovered. ***Look inside!***

Every year at Christmas there is a gift under the tree with a tag, **To: Krista, From: Krista.** I started this years ago to be funny. I was shopping for my family and found something I wanted, not necessarily needed. I knew no one would buy it for me, simply because no one knew I wanted it. I did not know I wanted it, until the moment I saw it. It has morphed into a standing Christmas joke. Other members participate now and then and we find it quite comical.

While coaching one day, my intuition showed me a To: Krista, From: Krista gift. The client was looking everywhere for what he needed, not knowing he had everything he needed inside of him. As best I could, I drew a gift box with a bow and a tag that said To: _____, From: _____. I asked my client to fill in his name, and then handed him the sheet of paper, with a question. What gift can you give yourself?

WHY, as Simon Sinek says, ***are you here?*** What is your purpose? It is exciting to discover and define your values, to know what you believe in, and to discover your gifts. However, the power of these is lost without a purpose. Where do you use what you have? How can you impact the world?

Most of us are not gifted with the ability to change the world with one unique creation. We are given the ability to touch the hearts, souls and lives of individuals daily. Don't lose sight of your gifts by looking for the big *'thing.'* Look inside for the little things that create big impacts.

"Keep Off My Grass!" Are your boundaries set? Are they clear? Boundaries are mental, emotional, physical and spiritual. Your values, beliefs and gifts have a voice in your boundaries. Nothing depletes your energy tank faster than others impeding upon your boundaries. Nothing drains you of hope faster than others impeding upon your boundaries. Boundaries are where you begin and where you end, and where others begin. ***Your boundaries are defined by you, and only you. You belong to you!*** Your mental, emotional, physical and spiritual boundaries, when held, fuel your soul. A healthy soul fuels your hope.

Who's measuring stick are you living by? If you have defined your values, know your beliefs, embrace your gifts, have clarity of purpose, own solid boundaries and carry a full energy tank, then what are you using to measure your success? ***STOP! Don't look out there!*** Look inside. Your success is measured through alignment. Alignment with who you are. Alignment with your values, beliefs, gifts, purpose and boundaries. This is your measuring stick and the fuel for your energy tank. Do not let others define your measuring stick. It is not others to define. You belong to you. You were created uniquely you. You define your success, and measure its progress. Every component on your measuring stick is at the core, your soul. Look inside.

Lead Who You Are.

There is only one you. Let the world have you. Your mere presence touches the hearts and souls of others. It is about moving your story forward. What if your story, you, triggered action in others? What if your story, you, stopped action in others? What if your story lived on for years? What if your story became the inspiration for change, creation, beliefs? ***What if?***

Walk with purpose and presence every day. Be present in everything you do. Contribute in every way you can. It is about giving and receiving. I have yet to figure out how to give and not receive. If I am present in my giving, I receive.

When I meet people, I continually hear, *"I have never met a life coach before. What do you do?"* I respond with, *"My purpose is to improve the world, one person at a time, by helping individuals become a better version of themselves."* Then, I wait for their eyes to gloss over. If they don't, then I know a connection is forming, and I continue. *"I take individuals through an inside-out journey of discovery thy self, know thy self, grow thy self, and lead thy self. My experience has shown me when individuals go through the inside-out journey they become better employees with you or for you, they become better participating members and leaders in their families, and they become better participating members and leaders in their community. Hence, with the gifts I have been given, I help improve the world one person at a time."*

It is not flashy, not sexy, and it won't put me in the headlines. It is what I was created to do.

I cannot be anyone other than who I was created to be. Oh, and I fought it for years. It was not my vision of my future. It was not other's vision of my future. It was not what I thought I was good at. It was not what others saw me as good at. It was not going to make me enough money. What a hoot! Me thinking I could create my own path, or change the path that had been set for me. All those years of trying to, or wanting, to be something I was not created to be.

WAKE UP! The journey is part of your gift to others. It has armed you with the skills, and given you the gifts, to make the world a better place. Get quiet, get present and listen. You will be amazed what your inside brings into view on the outside.

Use Who You Are. You are Enough!

Every day you make deposits and withdrawals in the world. At the end of the week, I always hope my deposits are larger than my withdrawals.

Growing up, my father was a man of few words, but when he spoke people listened. I do not remember the exact circumstance, but I do remember standing in the tool shed when he looked at me and said, *"If you can lay your head on your pillow at night and feel good about how your lived the day, then you lived it right. If you cannot feel good about how you lived the day, then the first thing you do tomorrow is right your wrongs."* **Shazam!**

You are enough! Are you using all of you? Are you giving your gifts to others? Are you making the world a better place? If not, right your wrongs.

I am confident my father's words were meant for a specific purpose that has slipped my mind, but they fit many aspects of our lives. My mother continually asked, *"What are you doing to make the world a better place for those who follow behind you?"*

You are here to leave and to serve. Leave pieces of you and to serve others. To strengthen souls so hope can be seen and felt. You are fuel for hope in the world. Do not over complicate or underestimate your gifts. Simply let your light shine while you leave and serve.

This little light of mine, I'm going to let it shine,
Oh, this little light of mine, I'm going to let it shine.
This little light of mine, I'm going to let it shine,

let it shine, let it shine, let it shine.

Every day, make a deposit to the world. Be contagious in serving others. Touch the heads, hearts and souls of those in your little corner of the world. You may just be the fuel to their soul that gives them to vision to see hope. **Look inside, shine outside.**

Leave Who You Are. The Butterfly.

Part of my frustration is not knowing, not being able to see if or what my impact has been. I like to start and finish my tasks. Heck, I have yet to see or understand exactly what I am supposed to do with the gifts I have been given. Okay, I am sure, I am unaware of all the gifts I have been given. I am still blind to, what I believe, are gifts I don't have.

I like to check tasks off my list and move on. For a time, I was frozen in place. I could not get anything checked off my list. I was frustrated. I did nothing. On this journey of mine, I am not given the luxury of always knowing or seeing my impact. Neither will you. You must be confident you are using your gifts in the way you were created to be. Be okay not knowing, but do not let this stop you from doing. There are lives that need your touch, a piece of you, to fuel their soul, ignite that fire in their belly.

Every action you take, every word you speak ripples for generations. What you leave touches the souls of others and ignites hope. In the words of Andy Andrews, The Butterfly Effect;

"How many generations forward, can we go, to see the lives you have touched? There are generations unborn, who's very lives will be shaped and shifted by what you do tomorrow, and the next day, and the next, and the next and the next. Because everything you do matters. Every move you make, every action you take, not just for you, not just for your family, not just for your home town. Everything you do matters to all of us, and forever."

People have told me I am motivational. I don't want to be motivational. I believe motivation comes from the outside and is short lived. Much like an energy drink consumed to give you a boost. What happens when the energy drink wears off? Most often, you end up with less energy than before you consumed the drink.

I want to be inspirational. I believe inspiration comes from the inside, the depths of you. Inspiration is rooted in your soul and woven into the fabric of who you are. Inspired people see more than what is right in front of them. When inspiration comes out, it fuels hope, and you see and believe things you are blind to in other moments. Inspiration resides inside all of us. Whether we tap into it is our choice. Helen Keller says; *the only thing worse than being blind is having sight but no vision.* Inspiration and vision walk together.

I believe our path in life is set, long before we are born. In the universe setting our path, we are given gifts. Gifts we are to use to make the world a better place. And by world, I mean your little corner of the world in which you reside. You are not meant to hold onto these gifts. They are called gifts, because they are meant to be given willingly to others. How you bring your gifts to the world is unique to you and is decided by you. The world needs what you have. Your gifts are the fuel to the souls of others, and strong souls ignite hope.

Hope is, because of your soul – Your soul is, because of hope

Look Inside to See Outside

STRATEGIES FOR IGNITING YOUR FIRE OF HOPE

You were put on this earth to serve others and to leave a part of you; to shape the world.

1. How are you making the world better for those who follow behind you?

_____

_____

_____

_____

2. What gifts have you been given to share with the world?

_____

_____

_____

_____

3. WHY are you here? What is your purpose?

_____

_____

_____

_____

4. In what way can you adjust your life, to live who you were meant to be?

_____

_____

_____

_____

5. If you changed one aspect of your being, that allows you to show up, who you are at the core, what would that one thing be?

_____

_____

_____

_____

ABOUT KRISTA MORRISSEY

Krista Morrissey is the Chief Growth Officer at *CHOICES Coaching & Consulting.* She is a professionally certified Life and Leader Coach through the International Coaching Federation, a public speaker and an organization development specialist. Krista has over two decades of domestic and international experience in a $4.5 billion-dollar company with over 25,000 employees worldwide. Krista is an adjunct instructor for the School of Business at Waukesha County Technical College, where she also serves on the Advisory Board for the Supervisory Management and Quality Management programs. In addition, Krista holds practitioner certifications for Franklin Covey, Myers-Briggs Type Indicator, Project Management, Master Lean Facilitator and Emotional Intelligence, and a Master of Adult Education with a specialty in Organization Development from Alverno College.

Besides coaching and working with organizations, Krista designs, hosts and facilitates Growth Camps and retreats around topics that are provocative, thought provoking and inspirational. When speaking to organizations, groups or at conferences, the audience is brought out of their seats and into the topic. There is no sitting on the sidelines when Krista is in the room.

Contact Krista:

- Website: www.ChoicesCoachingConsulting.com
- LinkedIn: www.LinkedIn.com/in/KristaMorrissey
- Facebook: www.Facebook.com/ChoicesCoachingConsulting
- Email: Krista@ChoicesCoachingConsulting.com
- Phone: 262-442-4303

SAVED BY A SONG

By Eden Adaobi Onwuka

SAVED BY A SONG

**There is no Co-pay for Hope,
The Tiniest Hope is better than dope.**

As I lay on a stretcher in a dark hospital room, I tried to relax unsuccessfully. A weak beam of light from the computer screen and the ultrasound machines was the only illumination visible to me. A nurse propped my head with pillows and covered me with a warm blanket. She tried to make small talk as I got half undressed. I reluctantly had to admit to myself that this time I was afraid. A deep gnawing dread that left me tossing and turning the previous night, unable to get much sleep. And though I tried to pass it off as nerves, it wasn't true. I knew the difference between rattled nerves, butterflies, anxiety and fear. This thing I felt was naked fear; a dark brooding trepidation that almost made me question everything I had ever known about healing and miracles.

The doctor soon walked into the room. She was beautiful with a warm smile and a kindness about her eyes that seemed to say to me, *"Hey, I know how you feel, I'll try to be gentle."* At that point, I exhaled a bit. She spoke calmly to me explaining what the procedure would entail while re-assuring me that it would be quick, painless though I would feel some pressure. She asked if I had any thoughts about the information I just received. I looked at her helplessly and asked the implication of the results returning back as positive. She explained that if the reports came back positive, it meant that the cancer had metastasized. Metastatic cancer, two words which held an ominous threat.

How did I get here, I silently wondered, recalling how three months ago, I received a phone call that changed everything. Barely nine months after giving birth to twin babies I noticed a lump in my breast and scheduled a wellness checkup. In a series of unfolding events much like flipping pages in a fast-moving plot, I made an appointment with a breast specialist then got biopsied and received the stunning news, *"Ms. Onwuka, sorry to inform you that your results came back for cancer."*

The doctors were concerned about the *"grade"* of the cancer and considered it to be aggressive. Totally blindsided, I grappled with feelings of confusion, surprise and anger; a likely cocktail of emotions those who receive an unexpected diagnosis have to deal with. I also inadvertently had feelings of shame, yes shame. Not because having cancer is shameful, but because I was trying to defend God's image in my head to anyone else who might later learn of it. Like a devoted child, I was misguided in my thinking to believe that this diagnosis was going to look bad on God's *"resume,"* or look *"as if"* God was not mindful enough of me. Or else, how could I accept in my heart to be diagnosed with cancer soon after my babies were born. One of my reactions at the time was, but God, I'm not even forty yet! Why me? Did I go wrong somewhere? Did we not pray enough? Could you not have prevented this? Somehow, I had encouraged myself soon after and went beyond those energy depleting thoughts about a week later. I had reminded myself that my response or reaction would acerbate or mitigate the impact of this situation. I had a conversation with myself asking; *"Eden, if someone were to call you to talk to their friend who just received a cancer diagnosis, what would you say to them?"* So, I took my own counsel, swallowed my own pills and internalized the coaching I would have given to a stranger, a friend or a client. I said,

"This is tough, I kid you not but it can become a lot worse with negative emotions, denial and a bad attitude. Your perspective determines your narrative. What you magnify grows and what you simplify goes, or at least it loses its power to control your joy."

Instead I entered into thanksgiving not BECAUSE of the cancer, but IN SPITE of it. My praise had nothing do with everything being perfect, rather I counted my blessings; those things I already had like access to good healthcare, a supportive spouse, children, while praising in advance for those things I desired like good health, the right support and caregivers. Hebrew words for praise have several variants each with a distinct meaning, but one interesting variant *"Towdah"* means to praise in anticipation for what we hope to receive. And that was what I did because I believed that God could use this to birth a new purpose, perhaps weave a message of light to others who might need the encouragement I had received in my heart while in communion with my Heavenly father. But all this was three months earlier.

Surprisingly, here I was yet again, grappling with the same feelings I struggled with in the beginning. All because the cancer had stopped suddenly responding to the initial chemotherapy treatments. I was on my tenth chemo cycle of Taxol when I curiously felt heavier in the affected area. Choosing not ignore it, I spoke with the oncologist about it and he ordered a new set of ultrasounds which sadly confirmed that somehow in spite of chemotherapy, the lump had doubled in size, at an alarming 100% increase and the lymph nodes surrounding the area which had been benign at the beginning had become abnormally enlarged. So, they recommended fresh biopsies right in the middle of my treatment to be certain that this was not a case of progression into metastatic cancer.

The helplessness I felt on that hospital bed had now morphed into fear. Was this the final death sentence? What was the extent of its spread? Two days earlier, my friend Omo had graciously visited from Ohio and offered to drive me to visit my physician, Dr. Anderson. Omo tried to encourage me but I pretended the turn of events was not a big deal. However, as I waited for the doctor, I knew it mattered more than I had admitted. And it mattered because I didn't feel the usual reserve of strength I normally felt before every procedure. I struggled to find the peace, which for me was the biggest sign of God's presence in my walk with Him, and it seemed to elude me.

The past two months and the chemotherapy I received every Friday suddenly seemed like a waste. And the side effects, tiredness, nausea, headaches, insomnia and pain, even the suffering, seemed to have been senseless. What then was the point of it all, if we had gone back to square one? I wondered. It even seemed the prognosis was worse that it had been at the preliminary biopsy. Except this time, I was a tired warrior who had already depleted most of her strength in the journey. The bursting faith I had stirred up before the treatment begun, was fast running out, and I felt like a long-haul truck driver who had run out of gas.

I looked up at the doctor and said, *"Please could you give me a minute or two? I don't like how I am feeling, and because I am a person of Faith, it matters to me not to move forward with this procedure until I deal with these fears."* She asked if there was anything she could do to make it better. And I had one simple request:

"Could I please, I need to play my favorite worship song…"

I knew that if I surrounded the atmosphere with worship my spirit would become calm again. I knew if I lifted the name of Jesus, the storm I felt raging within would lose its threat. I knew that the aura of worship influences everything, and I if I dared in that moment to lift a banner of thanksgiving, as ironical as it sounded, my focus will move from my situation to God's promises.

The doctor nodded empathetically and said that was okay. I looked at her pleadingly as I explained to her that I had tried to get the music to play on my YouTube for the past thirty minutes while waiting in the lobby, but my cell network provider had poor coverage in the hospital building. She responded with a kind offer. How about I give her the name of the song and artist and she would search for it on her phone. She found the song and put in on replay. As tears of worship came rolling down my cheeks, the nurse gave me a towel to cover my eyes. In that darkness, I saw a picture of a grim future, of pain, of death and devastation then the image turned around. With the rising up of worship in that hospital room, I began to feel the fear falling off, as the music *What a Beautiful name* by Hillsong United saturated the atmosphere:

> *"You didn't want heaven without us*
> *So Jesus, you brought heaven down*
> *My sin was great, your love was greater*
> *What could separate us now*
>
> *What a beautiful Name it is*
> *What a beautiful Name it is*
> *The Name of Jesus Christ my King*
>
> *Death could not hold You, the veil tore before You*
> *You silenced the boast, of sin and grave*
> *The heavens are roaring, the praise of Your glory*
> *For You are raised to life again"*

The biopsy procedure began as I lost myself in worship. I immersed myself in the truth that death held no power before the Almighty. My faith once again, came alive and I prayed fervently that God would reverse the cancer's path, that it would not progress into metastatic cancer. I declared His healing over my life and told myself repeatedly that He has not given me the spirit of fear, but of power, love and a sound mind. (2 Tim 1:7) And the song kept playing on and on. It was a song I had played from the beginning of the cancer treatment and at every juncture. I played it from the port placement to the first biopsies and the weekly chemotherapies. It held a deep meaning for me, and at odd times when on the way to the hospital or if I became anxious, the song popped up on KSBJ radio, the timing and co-incidence nothing short of divine.

I finally found the strength to manage a weak smile because there was a shift going on in me. It seemed like it was not just the biopsy but an exchange of spirits. I felt the comfort and assurance of God's presence I had longed for fill me up and I felt the peace I had searched for. The biopsy ended, and the medical staff left the room for a few minutes.

In that instant, something else happened. The song track somehow flipped onto to next track even though it had been put on replay and rather than change it, I chose to listen to this new unfamiliar song, and these words filtered through:

"When You don't move the mountains, I'm needing You to move
When You don't part the waters, I wish I could walk through
When You don't give the answers, As I cry out to You
I will trust, I will trust, I will trust in You"

I felt a warmth I could not explain and started laughing. It was so apt, the words captured exactly my present needs and gratitude filled my heart. With my favorite familiar song, God had restored my faith again and by the lyrics of an unfamiliar song God had moved me from the place of faith to the place of trust. It no longer mattered in that moment what the results would be, because I knew in my heart that God only held in His heart the best for me. I knew that His purpose was more important than my reality. And though I wanted to be healed, His character was not on trial. He was still a God of Love to me. And with that I entered into rest.

Many times, in life, we use conditions to gauge the love of a God who is limitless. We condition him with our broken humanity and our desperate conditions, *"God, if you heal my child..."*, *"If you give me a spouse..."*, *"If you help my friend break that addiction..."*, *"If this goes away..."*...Then I will serve you, for instance. But God desires to do a work within us that is greater than the work around us. To put a structure in us that withstands the turmoil before us. The empty, tired, scared, helpless woman who came into that hospital room for her biopsy was now the strengthened, peaceful, hopeful and trusting woman who got up from the hospital bed and it had nothing to do with the results. I still had no clue what the results would even be, since we had to wait a few days for the results to be out.

**Faith focuses on the Outcome,
Trust focuses on who we Become.**

I stood up joyful, not necessarily happy because happiness is transient and is based on happenstance, data, information, feelings, events and people. But I had joy, the joy I felt was from above. It came from looking within, at the faithfulness of God in times past, of His goodness from times before. Faith was good, yet without trust, faith could be depleted, and without faith, there will be no hope. My hope was revived with a song of praise, and this song carried me on through the next few months of intensified chemotherapies, the loss of hair, darkened skin, heart palpitations, shattering spines, dizzy spells, blackened broken nails, bleeding gums, neuropathy, hot flashes and through segmented mastectomy, radiation, physical therapies and hormonal therapy that may last the next few years.

**And Though we may feel helpless,
We must never become Hopeless.**

A few days later, the hospital called with good news. The cancer was not spreading. I was thankful for that. More importantly, I was thankful for **Faith, Trust and Hope**. I was later to learn that the song by Hillsong United was released on January 6, 2017 a day before I got my cancer diagnosis. I jokingly tell my friends that God let them make that song because He knew it would become my covenant anthem throughout this journey.

For someone reading this, there may be nothing worth celebrating in your life right now, but look again within and stir your joy. Joy flows from a decision to trust a dependable God with undependable circumstances. Find your joy, there's always a tiny trickle left hidden somewhere in gratitude. Find your song, it might be in a life that inspires, a phase, in nature, in the innocence of a child, in the foolishness of your mess, in your spouse, but your song will connect you to strength. It will lead you, like David's harp in the path of stilled waters. It will calm you, like David's Psalms as he ran from Saul. Your song will move you from a place of fear to faith and steady you to trust, and therein you'll find hope again.

*"And hope does not put us to shame, because God's love has been poured out
into our hearts through the Holy Spirit, who has been given to us."*
Romans 5:5 (NIV)

Footnote: *"What a Beautiful Name"* is a song released by the Australian praise and worship group Hillsong Worship. It is included in the album, *"Let There Be Light."* The song was led and written by Brooke Ligertwood, and was co-written with Ben Fielding. *"Trust in You"* is a song by Lauren Daigle, co-written with Michael Farren and Paul Mabury from the album *"How Can It Be."*

STRATEGIES FOR IGNITING YOUR FIRE OF HOPE

1. What has Adversity taught you? Have there been a lesson to learn in your silent seasons?

_____

_____

_____

_____

2. What quality(ies) helped you to overcome it?

_____

_____

_____

_____

3. What daily affirmations and conversations do you have with yourself? Would you include any from this story? If Yes, which ones?

_____

_____

_____

_____

_____

_____

4. What commitment are you willing to make to protect your Joy?

_____

_____

_____

_____

ABOUT EDEN ADAOBI ONWUKA

Eden Adaobi Onwuka is an International John C. Maxwell Certified Speaker and Trainer who delivers keynote speeches, and coaching to aid personal and professional growth through study and practical application of John's proven Leadership methods. With extensive leadership experience and the privilege of being mentored by some of the finest leaders, she believes no task is too mundane and no goal too magnificent. She holds degrees in Bachelor of Arts and humanities, and a Masters in Business Administration. Her corporate industry experience spans 15 years in e-commerce and financial services.

She is the Initiator of *Adopt A Widow* (A.A.W), a grassroots benevolence project aimed at providing annual support to bereaved women beyond their grief period. She loves volunteering, traveling and writes under a variety of genres from leadership, inspiration to short stories. She is widely known for her thought provoking nuggets, reflective one-liners and by the Brand name #SpeakerTrainerSage.

She is the Author of *"The Power of a Single Story,"* a collection of faith based short stories and *"I am More than Body Parts,"* a riveting memoir of courage and hope chronicling her journey to overcoming cancer.

She lives in Texas with her husband and three beautiful children.

Contact Eden:

- Website: www.EdenOnwuka.com
- Facebook: www.Facebook.com/EdenOnwuka
- Instagram: www.Instagram.com/UnwrittenSage

HOPE: PAIN INTO PURPOSE

By Edward Reed

HOPE: PAIN INTO PURPOSE

For centuries hope has been a powerful driver influencing attitudes and expectations of people throughout the world. While intangible, the impact of our choices affect ourselves and others. Have you ever met a person or been the person who lost hope? How does a person's sense of hopelessness impact relationships and productivity? You see, hopelessness robs us from developing our imagination and can send us into a downward spiral of negativity. When we lack hope, we accept limitations that others refuse to accept. Spectators often wonder, how people dealing with the same life circumstances can have very different outcomes. One of my favorite poems is by Chuck Swindoll called, *"Attitude."*

> *"The longer I live, the more I realize the impact of attitude on life. Attitude, to me, is more important than facts. It is more important than the past, than education, than money, than circumstances, than failures, than successes, than what other people think or say or do. It is more important than appearance, giftedness or skill. It will make or break a company...a church...a home. The remarkable thing is we have a choice every day regarding the attitude we will embrace for that day. We cannot change the inevitable. The only thing we can do is play on the one string we have, and that is our attitude... I am convinced that life is 10 percent what happens to me, and 90 percent how I react to it. And so, it is with you...we are in charge of our Attitudes."*

Over the years, I've had the privilege of helping others examine their current situation and see things from multiple perspectives. Perhaps the saddest situation I have encountered in my work is when people no longer see value in themselves and decided the only option to deal with their emotional response to their temporary situation is taking their life. I will never forget one night, while working at a residential crisis center for teens, a new resident attempted suicide on site. Our team quickly called the emergency medical team. I rode with the young person in the ambulance to the hospital. The short trip seemed like an eternity. As the sirens screamed going through traffic, I keep praying for God to save this precious child. The child was given another opportunity to find hope despite the hardships in her life. Hopelessness has the power to cast a dark shadow that blocks out the consideration of creative possibilities to address the challenges of life. Martin Luther King, Jr. eloquently stated, *"We must accept finite disappointment, but never lose infinite hope."*

When the storms of life hit understand it is only for a season. Anchor your hope for a better tomorrow by learning ways to become innovators of solutions. How do we avoid losing hope? Intentionally living life with a positive attitude equips us to create a vision for ourselves, families, communities and society that expects favorable outcomes regardless of circumstance. History has several examples of people who faced horrible circumstances and yet ignited by hope, they took action to produce favorable outcomes despite the challenges they encountered. George Washington Carver, explained, *"Where there is no vision, there is no hope."* What vision do you have for the areas of your life that are important to you? Are you looking at what already exist or the possibilities of what can come into existence? In life, we have those who create the stories of triumph that others talk about and those who stay trapped in the stories of being a victim. Hope has the power to turn tragedy into triumph.

One of my good friends and hope ambassadors, Marta Bota, is a true champion for others, strong in her faith and uses her influence to make a difference in the lives of others. As an ambassador for the Foundation Fighting Blindness, she inspires others through making speeches and raising funds for research into degenerative retinal disease. As an adult, Marta was diagnosed with Attention-Deficit/Hyperactivity Disorder (ADHD). In 2014, she founded the ADHD Help and Hope Network (www.Facebook.com/HelpNHopeNetwork), a Facebook community and repository of articles about symptoms and treatment, parenting strategies, classroom accommodations and products for people of all ages with ADHD. Children and Adults with Attention Deficit/Hyperactivity Disorder (CHADD), a national nonprofit education and advocacy group, named Marta an *"ADHD Champion."* Marta is a highly sought-after makeup artist, Ms. Virginia 2016, a dynamic wife and loving mother. She is also a presidential award winner for her community service.

In 2017, Marta shared a story with me about a dynamic young lady facing medical challenges who wanted to make a difference in the lives of tweens and teens. Marta and I share a passion to help make a difference in the lives of others as part of our calling. After hearing the young lady's story and watching her share words of hope and encouragement I committed to joining team Ashley.

Ashley is a 17-year-old with Ehlers-Danlos Syndrome (and a laundry list of comorbidities) who has spent a majority of her life in and out of hospitals, spending months at a time away from home, but all the while dreaming of ways to make things better for other patients. I have had the honor of joining Marta to spend time with Ashley in the hospital. Ashley's wisdom and spirit is incredible. In our time together, her insight makes me laugh and touches my heart in a special way. Her smile lights up the room. She is full of passion to bring hope and happiness to others despite her own suffering. According to Ashley, *"When you're stuck in the hospital and you don't feel well, it doesn't help if you don't look or feel like yourself – that's where makeup comes in."*

Children's hospitals rarely have activities or prizes for tween and teenage children; the focus is typically on the younger children. Like any normal teenage girl, Ashley loves makeup. During an eight month stay bouncing between Children's National Hospital and the local Ronald McDonald House, she created the idea of Warrior Glam Bags.

Each bag can be filled with different types of makeup, makeup brushes, nail polish, mini facial cleansers and more - all new for sanitary and safety reasons. The idea is to help each girl feel more like herself by being able to experiment and play with the makeup in these glam bags, helping each girl show her beauty that lies within. Ashely often says, *"How a girl feels about herself is extremely important. There is always beauty that lies within an illness."* As a dad with a daughter, I quickly learned the significance of style and image. Helen Keller once shared, *"Optimism is faith that leads to achievement. Nothing can be done without hope and confidence."* Not only is Ashley an amazing young lady, the story would not be complete without another amazing champion who has pulled Ashley under her angelic wings, Victoria Graham. When we humble ourselves and trust God's perfection in the midst of our own imperfection our hopes ignite our attitudes and action. Victoria sought out Marta to do Ashley's makeup for a photo shoot. Victoria is responsible for giving wings to Ashley's hope of impacting young ladies in the hospital.

Victoria is not a stranger to adversity and disappointment. Imagine being a 13-year old talented athlete and you became diagnosed with Ehlers-Danlos Syndrome (EDS) – after spending 3 years attempting to find out why you didn't feel well, listening to doctors accuse you of *"faking it,"* and *"making it up."* What would you do?

Victoria kept pushing forward, determined not to be sidelined by her medical situation. She played division III women's soccer and lacrosse for a small college where she pursued studying medicine. In 2013, she was the leading scorer for both teams and recognized as 2nd team All-Conference for the Middle Atlantic Athletic Conference for lacrosse as a freshman.

Adversity entered Victoria's life as she began experiencing loss of feeling in her limbs that her doctors couldn't explain then, in October 2013, she experienced a memory lapse that then began affecting her grades. After working with specialist, Victoria was diagnosed with Chiari Malformation and severe craniocervical instability and atlanto-axial instability. Her condition required brain and spinal surgery to attempt to resolve her condition.

As a strong woman of faith and leader on her teams, she wanted to help her teammates understand her situation. In an attempt to make them feel at ease (initially) Victoria quoted Jeremiah 29:11 *"'For I know the plans I have for you,' declares the Lord, 'plans to prosper you and not to harm you, plans to give you a hope and a future.'"* Remaining hopeful, she put her trust in her medical team's ability to help her.

As one surgery turned into two, she returned to school and drastically declined and needed a third surgery by the end of the year. Disappointment soon found a home in her life. Victoria began to doubt everything in her life, including herself, and found hope in Jeremiah 29:11.

Her journey consisted of surgery after surgery. Throughout this process, friendships began to fade away and the reality of what were once good intentions became broken promises of support. Life was not turning out the way she envisioned. Her faith was definitely tested and she began to lose hope. Psalms 94:19 (NLT) states, *"When doubts filled my mind, your comfort gave me renewed hope and cheer."* Despite her current situation, God had a different plan for Victoria.

Victoria transitioned from the world of sports into the world of pageantry. Realizing that there were other girls and other people out in the world who were in similar conditions as she was. She began pageants as something to cross off her *"bucket list."* Sometimes we can be recharged in odd situations. For Victoria, it was a photographer who sparked a bit of hope in her by asking to photograph her in her neck brace. She thought he was crazy, but the photo ended up reigniting her hope. This was the first photo where she began to see her true beauty.

It is important to understand that God puts His people in your life for reasons beyond what we see in the beginning of our relationships with them. This was the case for Victoria. God connected Marta and Victoria together. They met at a photoshoot where Marta and the photographer volunteered to help her create a visual ad campaign to *"Make Invisible Illnesses Visible."* The apostle Paul wrote in Hebrews 6:19 (NLT), *"This hope is a strong and trustworthy anchor for our souls. It leads us through the curtain into God's inner sanctuary."* Little did Marta and Victoria know, God had bigger plans than a photoshoot for the two of them.

Over the course of three years, Victoria endured ten brain and spinal neurosurgeries and countless other procedures. In 2016, in the midst of these surgeries, she noticed a huge need for support for patients with EDS and their families. Seeking to make a difference, she approached a few organization about ways they could work together to fill this gap and no one was interested. Victoria didn't realize at that moment, God prepared her to stand in the gap.

In April 2016, she decided that if no one was going to help these patients, she would. For her 22nd birthday, with no degree, she poured her life savings into creating a 501(c)(3) non-profit organization, The Zebra Network (www. TheZebraNetwork.org), which would work to increase education, promote advocacy and awareness, and provide support for Ehlers-Danlos Syndrome and associated comorbidities. In October 2016, she won the title of Miss Frostburg with the Miss America Organization where she held an educational platform entitled, *"But You Don't Look Sick"* – Making Invisible Illnesses Visible.

Despite her health challenges, disappointment with broken promises of support by former friends, and internal struggles with hope, Victoria never let go of God's hand. Her faith and determination took the same top scorer on the athletic field and made her a top scorer on God's field. During her year of service, she visited a few hundred kids in the hospital; lobbied on Capitol Hill for rare, chronic, and invisible illnesses, and served at nearly 250 events. In early 2017, her personal story was picked up by Babble and BBC, it then went viral across the world into thirty countries and was translated into eight languages. Victoria became known as the *"beauty queen with a twenty-five inch scar."* Through her platform, people began to learn about Ehlers-Danlos Syndrome.

Hebrews 11:1 (NLT), *"Faith shows the reality of what we hope for; it is the evidence of things we cannot see."*

During my conversation with Victoria, she shared, *"This was especially important to people who have EDS because it was finally being recognized and justified. It led many to find hope because they could show friends – hey, that's what I have and it was a story of a girl who was achieving with having a debilitating illness. I was ok with sharing my story because it meant that people could think 'I can do it, because she can.' I aim at being a living example and now run very transparent social media that shows my good days and bad days (and, yes, people have recognized me in random places like Starbucks and Marshalls) – but it is all WORTH IT."*

Some say, God has a funny sense of humor and a special way of forming teams to move His agenda forward. God is so incredible, He brings people from various backgrounds and social circles together. Victoria *"met"* Ashley sometime in 2017 from a mutual *"little sister"* (friend) who also has EDS. Victoria asked Ashley what her favorite things were, she said raising awareness and makeup. Don't miss it. Victoria and Ashley share a common love to help others. Victoria spent time with Ashley and decided to surprise her with a makeover and photoshoot. Victoria knew Marta's compassion for uplifting others and gifted hands as a makeup artist. This is how the three came together.

On the stage, Victoria often will tell her audience, *"Some of my biggest take away is that every single person has an obstacle that they must overcome. How you face that obstacle often dictates the outcome. No, being positive and hopeful will not cure my incurable, untreatable illness, but it might make every day a little brighter and better. Every morning you have a choice, to fight or to drown in your own tears. You have to fight. You just have to because there is a great a plan for you and I truly believe that the Lord does not put us through tribulations without the promise of a great future. Many people ask me how I do it and I always answer, 'I don't know' because the reality is that it is not my doing. The Lord helps me and he is the one who gets me through it. I have a faith that the Lord has plans to give me a hope and a future. I hope, I have faith, and I believe."*

God knew what He was going to do with His three angels before they even know each other. Marta, Ashely and Victoria have lived very different lives and represent different generations yet their faith, hope and love have come together to form a braid anchored in God. I am blessed to serve and share a bond with these three wonderful ladies as siblings in Christ. Together, we share a deep desire to encourage, equip and empower others driven by the greatest commandment, Jesus replied: *"Love the Lord your God with all your heart and with all your soul and with all your mind.' This is the first and greatest commandment. And the second is like it: 'Love your neighbor as yourself.'"* (Matthew 22:37-39).

God provides each of us the opportunity to turn pain into purpose. We have the freedom to share our experiences with others in a way to encourage them to be hopeful. Living in an imperfect world directly challenges hope. Putting your faith into a perfect God gives us the justification to be hopeful. Perhaps there is someone in your circle of influence that would benefit from hearing your story. Who is that person? What is preventing you from taking action to be a blessing to someone the Lord has put on your heart? Sometime, the person who needs to experience your love and compassion is the one staring back at you in the mirror.

My prayer for you, *"Dear God, thank you for both pain and pleasure. Provide me with insight, wisdom, compassion and provisions to be a blessing to others and myself. Help me discern the hearts and motivation of those who have come into my life. Help me move beyond my regrets and embrace my opportunities. Help me clearly understand my purpose and see the vision. Strengthen me when my hope waivers. Thank you. In Jesus name. Amen."*

The apostle Paul wrote, in 1 Corinthians 13:13 (NLT), *"Three things will last forever—faith, hope and love—and the greatest of these is love."*

STRATEGIES FOR IGNITING YOUR FIRE OF HOPE

1. How does your attitude impact your hope in tough times?

_____

_____

_____

_____

2. What is your vision for yourself in the next 6 months?

_____

_____

_____

_____

3. What are your top 3 barriers attempting to hold you back from achieving your desired outcomes?

_____

_____

_____

_____

4. What lessons of hope did you learn as you read the stories of Ashley and Victoria?

_____

_____

_____

_____

5. Take a few days and write out an outline of your story. Who can you share your story with? I would love to hear your story, send me an email with your story.

_____

_____

_____

_____

_____

_____

_____

6. What are some simple ways you can turn your hope into action items?

_____

_____

_____

_____

7. Create a hope into action journal for the next 12 months. On Sunday, write down something you hope to achieve for the week. List out the action steps necessary to accomplish your desire. Next implement your steps and record your outcomes at the end of the week.

_____

_____

_____

_____

ABOUT EDWARD REED

Ed Reed is a humble leader, who overcame challenges, setbacks, and other barriers that typically prevent people from living a life of significance. Ed credits his success to his faith, parents, professors, mentors and coaches for equipping him with the skills and mindset necessary for beating the odds of attaining success. For more than 25 years, Ed has successfully lead, empowered and coached students, parents, aspiring leaders, professionals, executives and leadership teams. Ed is the founder and CEO of *Academic Management Group, LLC* – a small business that provides coaching, strategic educational and career planning, consulting, personality and career interest assessments, and leadership development training services. Ed is a certified John C. Maxwell International Executive Coach, Leadership Trainer and Keynote Speaker. Ed believes people are the most valuable resources in every organization and that cultivating a culture of leadership is critical to long-term organizational success. His coaching and leadership training focuses on empowering and equipping people to effectively connect with others, stretch beyond their comfort zone, and apply sound wisdom to build their foundation for long-term success. His passion is visible when he is developing leaders of all ages to become critical thinkers, collaborators and problem solvers.

Contact Edward:

- Website: www.AcademicManagementGroup.com
- Website: www.JohnMaxwellgroup.com/EdwardReed
- Facebook: www.Facebook.com/AcademicManagementGroupLLC
- Twitter: www.Twitter.com/EReedSpeaks
- Email: EReed@AcademicManagementGroup.com
- Phone: 301-335-6689

HOPE AND FEAR CANNOT OCCUPY THE SAME SPACE

By Janea Trapp

HOPE AND FEAR CANNOT OCCUPY THE SAME SPACE

"Hope and fear cannot occupy the same space. Invite one to stay."
Maya Angelou

In 2016, I celebrated my 20th class reunion. It was a special time for me. I was asked to give the keynote message, *"Living a Life of Significance,"* in the high school auditorium. It was an amazing time of hope and optimism as I realized a dream I had as a young student sitting in that very auditorium years ago, to someday be on stage, delivering a message that would reach people and have the ability to change their lives. Years ago, our high school class listened to a young woman tell her very personal story about contracting HIV. She spoke about how life had changed for her, and how she initially felt sorry for herself, but as she spoke, her message changed to one of courage and determination. She shared how she soon discovered that she was called to share a message of hope in the midst of fear. Although she had no idea what the future would hold for her, she was choosing to spread a message of education and hope across the country by speaking to junior and senior classes. I learned that day that **FEAR** and **JUDGMENT** exist in the absence of **HOPE** and **KNOWLEDGE**. I have no idea where this woman is today, or if her illness has since called her home to be with God, but to this day, I continue to think about her, and how she placed in my heart the desire to speak and encourage others.

To be honest, even at a young age, I would sit there in awe during school assemblies and think to myself...someday...someday, I want to do that! So, the **BIG** day was quickly approaching. I must have written what I wanted to say a dozen times. I would put it aside, come back and inevitably toss it out and start over. I wanted so much for my message to be perfect and let's face it, I wanted to look good and successful. So, there I was driving back to my hometown on a Friday evening with my 6-year-old son, Noah, in the back seat. I must have been mumbling to myself because he asked, *"Mom, what did you just say?"* I didn't respond, and a few moments later, I hear, *"Mom, what are you talking about? I can't hear you."* And there you have it, I began confessing to my child that I was nervous, afraid, and I still had no idea what I was going to talk about. Young children are truly amazing because their answers are so sincere and simple. At the end of my rant, filled with self-doubt and uncertainty, Noah simply said, *"Mom, I would just tell them about what you've learned."* Placing the fear of being judged aside, I was proud of the message that I delivered.

Living a life of significance does not come naturally to many of us. One must be authentic and true to the purpose for which God created us to live a life of significance. As children and young adults, we are filled with ideas, hopes and dreams. How sad it is that life quickly conforms so many of us, and we find ourselves sacrificing our relationships with God, family and friends. We become so focused on the next pay increase or promotion that putting in hours of overtime seems to take priority over spending quality time with our spouse and children. I had a corporate job that I enjoyed, and I truly believed if I just tried a little harder or pushed a little more, my efforts would be recognized and rewarded. One of the first to arrive in the morning and generally one of the last to leave, I was no stranger to long hours. I wasn't taking care of myself spiritually, mentally or physically, and it eventually caught up with me. I was so unhappy that everything around me was suffering, including my job. I had to learn the hard way that I was chasing after an illusion of success, instead of becoming significant in the lives of those I cared about. I shared my struggles and feelings of unfulfillment with my supervisor with the hope that something would change, only to have my words used against me in an annual review. At my lowest point, I was so broken that no amount of *"hope"* was going to fix me. I felt nothing but shame and regret, and I just wanted it all to go away. Before I realized it, I was sharing with my peers about the night I wanted to die. Sharing this experience was difficult, and I wasn't sure if it was the right thing to do. We had lost a classmate to suicide our senior year, and many of his close friends were in the audience. I shared:

"God, I have made a complete mess out of things. I feel restless all the time and no matter how hard I try, it never seems to matter. I am not the wife my husband deserves, the mother my son needs or even the daughter of God I know in my heart You created me to be. Every day is a constant struggle. If this is all there is for me, please let me come home. I need You to bring me home. I cannot let my family know I gave up. I need You by my side to get through this."

The next morning, I woke up with a feeling of peace I had never experienced before. I knew God had me, and it would be okay. It was never about wanting to die; I just didn't want to live the unfulfilled life I had anymore. I felt, in that moment, that it was important to share a message that the absence of hope one day, cannot keep it from being renewed within you the next. To live a life of significance, we sometimes need to give a voice to our own struggles and setbacks. Each of us has experiences that have the power to inspire others, but our own pride often gets in the way of sharing those stories with the transparency needed to reach others. I literally screwed up, and the result was nothing short of a massive career setback. My actions resulted in the worse performance review of my career, and my supervisor informed me that Human Resources suggested that he work with me on a personal improvement plan.

It didn't happen overnight, but eventually, I allowed myself the opportunity to hope, believe and dream again. Whenever I felt hope slipping from my grasp, I would cling tighter to my faith. Instead of figuring things out on my own, I prayed and involved God more. I asked for His help and guidance. I would ask, *"What is it that You would have me do?"* As a result, doors began to open – doors that are waiting to open for you, if you let them. I made it a point to value, believe in and unconditionally love myself **EVERY DAY**, and I encourage you to start. Do this, and you will begin to see changes in those around you, as you will begin to value, believe in, and unconditionally love others as well.

Looking back, I can tell you that 2015 was a year of personal growth and awareness for me, and at its very core, was always a sense of hope. When we are able to hold on to hope and believe in and value ourselves, we should also invest in ourselves. Through investing in ourselves, we reaffirm hope daily in that we know something else is waiting for us. The prior experiences with that supervisor had me not only questioning a lot about myself, but I questioned his behaviors as well. I no longer trusted him with my personal growth and development. It was clear that my supervisor had written me off and was disinterested in helping me. I needed to seek out other resources and possible mentors, so I began reading books on leadership and self-improvement every night, and I continued to pray.

My prayers were answered when I happened to stumble across the John Maxwell Team, which provided me with learning opportunities that exceeded what I originally requested in my prayers. In early 2016, my weight loss coach asked if I would be interested in a job working as a coach. My corporate job was no longer a good fit for me. I wanted a flexible work schedule. It was not a decision I made lightly. It meant accepting a significant pay cut, and the only real benefit was the promise of controlling my schedule. In April 2016, I left my corporate job of nine and one-half years for the hope to build something of which I could be proud.

As I told this story to my classmates, I encouraged them to take chances and go after their dreams with courage and persistence. To strive each day to live a life of significance.

So much has changed in the year since I addressed my senior class. That September morning was a snapshot in time when life was falling into place, and I thought I knew exactly what the next year would bring. Two weeks later, everything would begin to change when we received a letter in the mail. The developer of our subdivision had gone bankrupt, and without a homeowner's association in place yet, the city mayor would now be making decisions regarding its development. Concerned about the investment we made into our home, with talk of duplexes and the possibility of apartments, we decided to place our home up for sale. We were blessed to sell quickly, and we moved into our new home December 31, 2016.

I'm not sure if the ink was even dry on the loan documents when I returned to work the following Tuesday to find out the medical practice would no longer be offering Ideal Protein, and going forward, my position there was in question. I was in total disbelief! I kept the news to myself for a few days, convinced I might be able to work with our office manager to change the doctor's mind. I seriously dreaded having to tell my husband because he had not been 100 percent on board with my decision to leave my corporate job. A week later, with my husband's support, I purchased the weight loss clinic. Everything happened so quickly that there was no time to really plan for anything or consider other options. Initially I continued to operate out of the family practice three days a week and worked as a front desk receptionist two days a week. Within a few months, this arrangement was no longer working. Afraid I would lose too many clients by moving the clinic to the town where I reside (30 minutes south of the current location), I chose to move my business into a chiropractor's office a few miles away. With this move I became 100 percent self-employed. The summer months proved to be difficult and challenging. I gained a client or two, just to lose another. I kept thinking about the vision I had when I decided to become a health coach, and it started keeping me up at night. My thoughts would then focus on how I could most effectively market and build a business on my own with little to no capital.

I sought the advice of other clinic owners, did some soul searching, and decided that I needed my business closer to home, in a smaller community where I could really focus my efforts. I was so excited — my own retail and office space! My current clients were all on board, and I even made arrangements to keep seeing some of them in the chiropractor's office once a week. This was going to work, right? I prayed long and hard, seeking God's guidance for signs that I was on the right path. I felt good about my decisions, and on October 1st, I took my biggest leap of faith yet, and signed a lease on my very own space. Now, we all know nothing goes according to plan, and circumstances being what they were, getting my new location ready for business took more money and time than I had planned. Then, two weeks into October, I lost four clients for various reasons and endured a number of missed appointments, all with no potential clients on the horizon.

Fear was setting in, and I found myself struggling just to finish this chapter. It's much easier to write about following your heart with hope and conviction when a struggle has ended and things are going well. It is quite another, to give and restore hope in others when your own hope is under attack. Then I realized maybe this is the message God wanted me to share. I have come to the conclusion that hope and fear coexist. Yes, in a book all about restoring hope I am going to tell you that fear is never far behind. Fear loves to lurk in the shadows of our hopes and dreams. It drives doubt into our hearts and minds, and succeeds when we let it overcome our thoughts and we begin to self-doubt. I have found myself in situations over the past few weeks where I have been so consumed by fear that I became completely paralyzed. It is in these situations that you must really dig deep, focus on your *"why,"* and know that for hope to survive, it must be tied to your faith. It is normal to feel uncomfortable and fearful at times. Anytime we push ourselves outside of our comfort zone, we will be met with obstacles and uncertainty. It is how we maneuver the obstacles and how we view uncertainty that makes the difference. Maya Angelou once said, *"Hope and fear cannot occupy the same space. Invite one to stay."* So, while hope and fear coexist in our day to day lives, we can intentionally choose **HOPE** over **FEAR**. We can be intentional in our choices of what we read and listen to, who we associate with and, most importantly, how we treat ourselves. Remember to value, believe and unconditional love who **YOU** are. When we do this, it becomes easier to not only keep hope alive within ourselves, but we are able to restore hope in others.

I am far from having everything figured out. When I look back on my experiences this past year, I know that I made more mistakes when my decisions were made from a place of fear rather than a place of hope. I believe God has given me opportunities to grow personally, professionally and even spiritually in His perfect timing. Trust that you just have to take that first step for God to know that you are ready and open to receiving all He has planned for you. Attach your faith to your hope and invite both to occupy your life to the point fear has no room to move in.

STRATEGIES FOR IGNITING YOUR FIRE OF HOPE

1. Have you found yourself bargaining with yourself between what you want, what you feel God wants and what society tells you, you should be or do?

_____

_____

_____

_____

2. Do you value, believe and unconditional love yourself? Do you value, believe and unconditionally love others? If not, how can you start?

_____

_____

_____

_____

3. When fear sets in, what are some things you can do to remain focused and hopeful?

_____

_____

_____

_____

ABOUT JANEA TRAPP

Janea Trapp is the owner/founder of a health and wellness company, *NuLife Insights Corporation*. A company focused on healthy lifestyle building and improving mindset through personal growth and development.

Corporate burnout, leading to a huge professional set back in 2014 was the catalyst necessary for Janea to begin her journey from employee to business owner. Through implementing her own personal growth plan, she became focused and intentional with who and how she spent her time. As a shift in mindset occurred physical health was next on the list. She sought out a program that provided her with education and weekly access to an accountability coach. In January of 2017, Janea purchased an Ideal Protein Weight Loss Clinic and operates it as part of *NuLife Insights*.

Janea is also a certified coach, speaker and trainer with the John Maxwell Team and enjoys speaking with groups about her ever-evolving transformational journey and lessons learned along the way. Janea believes that many of us have something that holds us captive from living the life we desire, but more importantly from living the life God created us for. Whether we are fortunate enough to discover this purpose or *"calling"* early in life or we stumble upon it in our later years, the journey is always unique and specific to that individual. Our lives constantly evolve and the journey only ends with our last breath. The key is to be intentional each and every day.

Contact Janea:

- Website: www.NuLifeInsights.com
- LinkedIn: www.LinkedIn.com/in/JaneaTrapp
- Facebook: www.Facebook.com/NuLifeInsights
- Email: Janea.Trapp@NuLifeInsights.com

THE REUNION – HOPE IS A CHOICE

By Carlos Vargas

THE REUNION – HOPE IS A CHOICE

"But while he was still a long way off, his father saw him and was filled with compassion for him; he ran to his son, threw his arms around him and kissed him."
Luke 15:20

One day while meditating I began thinking about the prodigal son. He was trying to follow his heart when he decided to venture out and discover the world. Many times the son is portrayed as a person who wanted to leave home to begin a life of sin. However, there is another side to the story. The prodigal son had a dream, a vision and he bravely wanted to follow it.

In Luke 15:12 the scriptures tell us that the father *"divided his property between them,"* which might indicate that the father understood his son's ambition. However, in Luke 15:13 it says, *"Not long after that the younger son got together all he had, set off for a distant country and there squandered his wealth in wild living."*

To avoid the pitfalls of sin, the prodigal son needed to develop and nurture six key values, which would be the basic ingredients to develop his hope. Those six ingredients include **character, endurance, humility, strength, dependence and tenacity.**

Sometime ago I was passing through a very difficult time in my life, even though to casual observers it might have appeared to be the best time in my life. I had lost all hope. I kept pushing, concentrated on improving my productivity at work, volunteering at church and doing wonderful things for God. But there was something missing. It was as my life was on autopilot. My soul was struggling. I could not pin point what was happening.

While praying and meditating one of my favorite author's quotes came to mind: *"Men are anxious to improve their circumstances, but are unwilling to improve themselves; they therefore remain bound."* James Allen from *As a Man Thinketh.* When that quote that came to me, I realized that much like the prodigal son, I needed to look to develop the same six values to regain my hope. Many times, people say put your hope in God, and that is true. We put our hope in God and

He gives us his word so we can understand what He wants for us. Lets look at what the prodigal son needed to develop to regain his hope.

Character

Character is an attribute that everyone must possess to identify where they are standing in relation to their convictions. Previously the prodigal son didn't develop his character because he had never had a need to do so. Everything was decided for him. It is said that character is revealed in the most difficult moments of life. Situations test us. Like the prodigal son, we must recognize that perhaps our character is not completely aligned with what our father wished for us. Character growth determines the height of personal growth. If your character isn't constantly growing you will not be able establish a healthy amount of hope in your life.

One of my mentors says: *"I will be better on the inside than I am on the outside."* John C. Maxwell. And that is so true. If I want to re-ignite my hope I need to realize that it is an inside job. It is completely dependent on my character as the first step and it is up to me to move to the next step.

Endurance

After the prodigal son squandered all his money, he was in need. I know that I can relate to this because in several times in my life I have not made the best decision in different areas of my life. It is very interesting that the story says, *"There was a severe famine in the whole country, and he began to be in need."* From wealthy to poor, it is an interesting change and drives home the point that the son needed develop the skills necessary to grow into the person that he was supposed to become. How many times have we traveled from one end of the equation to another? It is important to understand that in this life we will have to endure different situations. Jesus said in John 16:33: *"In this world you will have trouble. But take heart! I have overcome the world."* We must endure the process. And as the prodigal son when we are passing through challenging times, we learn to endure the process and develop the necessary wisdom for taking the next step.

Humility

Humility is another value that the prodigal son needed to develop, and the story tells us that his boss sent him to feed the pigs. Again, what a change from being a rich wealthy person to feeding pigs. Were any other job available? We are left to wonder if he couldn't have used his skills to get a better job than feeding the pigs? Perhaps, but when you are going through an inconvenient situation, you need to hit rock bottom in order to get back up. So many times, we experience similar situations. We may not end up feeding the pigs literally but it feels like we are. Nothing goes our way, we think everyone is against us and it is not until we realize that we need to humble ourselves and recognize that we are not in charge or on top. When we do that and humble ourselves our situations start to change. This step is very important because sometimes we have been wronged or a situation affect us we may take an attitude of a victim. Why me? I am so good. I am a great worker. When we humble ourselves, and recognize that everything is up to God, only then can He break the mold and recreate us into His image. The prodigal son needed to learn that he was not in control. In our life there are three situations that initiate change and humble ourselves. We may hurt enough, learn enough or receive enough that we are able to humble ourselves.

Strength

Often we think we are so strong and that we have the required skills to fight anything. But let me ask you a question, in your most challenging time, in that moment where you probably lost hope did you feel strong? Did you feel that you had everything under control? If you could look back at that moment were you at the top of your game or were you at the bottom of the pit? I would like to make a little confession, I have felt like the prodigal son wanting to get a little help, a little refresher for my life. However, it wasn't until I developed the strength needed to grow again that I was able to build myself back up. I learned from the prodigal son that when *"he longed to fill his stomach with the pods that the pigs were eating,"* the son was developing self-control. As a servant he was going to eat the food that was provided for the servants, but why did the bible provide this detail? Jesus always wanted to teach us something through parables. So many times, we expect something without exerting the effort required to receive what we want. For each one of us to rebuild our hope we need to put in the work required for it. Normally we expect that hope is something that is just given and easy. Hope for the best. Hope is not a strategy if you are not willing to put in the work and develop the strength required to fulfill your God given purpose on this earth.

Dependence

The next value that the prodigal son had to learn was dependence. At the beginning, he was depending on himself. He had money, friends, food, pleasures, but then he lost it all. In despair, realized that his father's servants had a better life than him. The son had to switch from thinking of what he could do by himself, to what his father could for him. It was an interesting shift. Abraham also experienced complete dependence on God when he was asked to sacrifice Isaac. And when Abraham learn and obediently depended completely on God's provision then it manifested in his life. In the same way, the prodigal son had to recognize I can't do this alone, I need my father and I will go back to him. We need to learn to depend completely on our heavenly Father. He will receive us and provide what we need so we can have the life that He intended for us.

Tenacity

The last value the prodigal son learned was tenacity. He had to experience the entire process and each step taught him something different. In Luke 15, verse 21 it says: *"I will set out and go back to my father and say to him: 'Father, I have sinned against heaven and against you. I am no longer worthy to be called your son; make me like one of your hired servants.'"*

Some people just want to get up without paying the price but the prodigal son teaches us that if we want to have hope we need to go through the process and be willing to go the distance. He was the son but he was willing to come back as a servant.

You and I are called to be like the prodigal son, to rebuild hope for a better tomorrow, to resolve difficult situations, to build new relationships and make tough choices.

Separation of Father and Son

The father knew that this was going to be an arduous process for the prodigal son, but it was a necessary step for the son's personal and spiritual growth. Chilean writer Isabel Allende asserts, *"I never said I wanted a 'happy' life but an interesting one. From separation and loss, I have learned a lot. I have become strong and resilient, as is the case of almost every human being exposed to life and to the world. We don't even know how strong we are until we are forced to bring that hidden strength forward."* The prodigal son's journey was going to be difficult but it was worth it. The father in the story is a representation of God the father and He will always protect us. In the book of Psalms 3:2-6 (NCV) says: *"Many are saying about me, 'God won't rescue him.' Selah but, Lord, you are my shield, my wonderful God who gives me courage. I will pray to the Lord, and he will answer me from his holy mountain. Selah, I can lie down and go to sleep, and I will wake up again, because the Lord gives me strength. Thousands of troops may surround me, but I am not afraid."*

The prodigal son was focused initially on his dream, but after his aspirations fell through he had to develop his hope to continue the journey. The journey of the thousand miles starts with one step, and the prodigal son needed to get up and start walking.

It is up to us if we want to develop our hope. In Mark Chapter 4, verses 30-34, Jesus compares our walk with a mustard seed. Why? Because we need to grow and develop. Time will not make us wiser or smarter. We need to take the steps to take our God given gifts and use them. Sometimes even when we have lost all hope, we need to rely on the truth of the word. Reading the word of God is the key for you to connect to the Father and develop hope.

We all go through tricky situations. We experience moments when we want to throw in the towel and forget about everything. That is okay, we are human and sometimes those moments come to us, but we must remember that our Father in heaven is our strength. He will help us to regain our strength and hope.

As I mention before, I have experienced times where I lost my hope. It felt awful. Do you want to know how I got my hope back? How I got my hope on?

My personality is a mix between the Apostle Paul and the Apostle Peter and that makes me a dominant/inspiring person. So my first challenge was recognizing that I needed some time to understand what was happening. I needed to take time to analyze what was happening inside of me, just like the prodigal son had some down time after his situation. Then I started to consider the source where God can spoke to me. It did not mean that I was far away from God, but I needed to go deeper in my reliance of His will. You too may need to go deeper in your relationship with Him. The word of God is key to providing the solutions. If I wanted to develop my hope in Him, I needed to understand, believe and practice what the Bible says. Here are some of the passages that directed me how to develop my hope.

- God is willing to protect us - Psalm 3:2-6

- God wants us to grow – Mark 4:30-34

- God wants us to get out of my comfort zone – Luke 18:35-43

- God will help us win against what looks impossible – 1 Corinthians 15:54-58

- God will see the outcome of his promise in us – Revelation 22:18-21

- God will bring the transformation needed in my life – Leviticus 26:4-45

- God is my GPS when I am in demanding situations – Joshua 10:25

- God will provide us better things than what I lost – 1 Peter 1:3-6

- God wants us to live in freedom not in bondage – Proverbs 13:12

- God created a process to develop hope – Romans 5:2-7

- God is with us, so I don't have to be afraid – Isaiah 41:10

- God will help us develop hope so I won't be discouraged – Joshua 1:9

- God has a plan for my prosperity – Jeremiah 29:11

- God wants us to put our trust on him – Psalm 71:5

A light shines in the darkness for honest and hopeful people, for those who are merciful and kind and good. It is good to be merciful and generous. Those who are fair in their business will never be defeated. Good people will always be remembered. Keep looking for hope, God will help you develop it and when you get it, be generous with it. Help others to have hope in God and in their future. And as the book of Romans 12:12 says: *"Let your hope keep you joyful, be patient in your troubles, and pray at all times."*

Hope is always a choice. Choose wisely.

STRATEGIES FOR IGNITING YOUR FIRE OF HOPE

1. What situation had you faced in life that separated you from reaching your purpose?

_____

_____

_____

_____

2. During life we may experience different levels of hope. If you can rate yourself from a 1 – 10 what is your level of hope right now?

_____

_____

_____

_____

3. Based on your answer from question #2. What will happen if your hope increases 1 or 2 numbers?

_____

_____

_____

_____

4. Thinking on your personal, professional or emotional relationship, which area in your life needs to be reunited with your heavenly Father?

_____

_____

_____

_____

5. Have you ever experienced a reunion similar to the prodigal son's in your personal or business life? What happened? What did you learn from it?

_____

_____

_____

_____

6. If you could change one thing that would increase your hope what would it be?

_____

_____

_____

_____

ABOUT CARLOS VARGAS

Living to Serve, Lead and be a Technical Geek.

For the last 20 years, Carlos Vargas has inspired people in numerous parts of the world, including Brazil, Mexico, the Dominican Republic, Paraguay, Cuba, Puerto Rico, the United States and Europe, to reach new levels with their lives through his God given talents of speaking and teaching. Carlos loves being a transformational agent for people who are struggling with limiting beliefs in their business, personal and spiritual lives. This is the fuel which keeps him going.

Carlos works with individuals, families, groups and businesses to introduce principles that reduce stress and help bring greater levels of happiness to their lives.

Carlos earned his education in the Defenders of the Faith Theological Institute in Santurce, Puerto Rico and later received over than 80 IT certifications during his successful career as an international architect with Fortune 100 and 500 companies.

Carlos was part of an elite team of world changers that was invited to travel to Paraguay and help transform the lives of 17,000 people.

As International Leadership and Life Coach, he finished a tour through the beautiful countries of Brazil and Cuba where he helped countless people transform their limiting beliefs into new opportunities.

Contact Carlos:

- Website: www.CarlosVargas.com
- Website: www.VIPLeadershipGroup.com
- Facebook: www.Facebook.com/cavarpe
- Facebook: www.Facebook.com/VIPLeadershipGroup
- Twitter: www.Twitter.com/Carlos_E_Vargas

BEING A WARRIOR OF HOPE

By Tricia Andreassen

BEING A WARRIOR OF HOPE

I realized something very powerful today as I took a few moments to sit in my private room and reflect. I am a warrior that stands for many missions. I have known for a while that the symbol of a warrior would be a big part of my life. Since my vision in 2016 (after my angel experience in 2015) at the mountain in Little Switzerland, North Carolina, the concept of being a warrior has been embedded in my spirit. I do need to write down and document my story. It is a powerful story of personal transformation.

As I made the final title selection for this book on Hope and reflected on the last four weeks of my life, I felt a voice inside encourage me. *"Tricia, you are a Warrior of Hope,"* it said. I never would have thought that specifically about myself, which in reflection may be considered weird since I have a private group called Warriors for Hope on Facebook. Still it took me all of this time to realize that I AM a warrior in every part of my DNA. Sure, I call myself Ms. Unstoppable, the Unstoppable Warrior, but me a Warrior of Hope? I thought I was the warrior who was a way-maker, the one who carved a path in the thickest woods to create a way for leaders to join together from all four corners of the world.

Even as I write this, I am visualizing a path that I have carved in the darkness that meets at a crossroads that intersects with other paths. It is the path traveled by other leaders that have felt the calling also to be way-makers in this mission to deliver what God wants.

So why now about this revelation being a Warrior of Hope? It is because I have had to fight at many times to find hope; to make sure hope was still there. I would be lying if I told you I always have hope because there have been times where the enemy has played with my mind saying many things to destroy. And, it still is a battle where I must pick up my sword to fight these words and feelings that go along with them:

"Everything is going to fall apart."

"You know that person who said it was all your fault? Well, it is. Look what a screw

up you are."

"You just make things worse."

"If you would just make more money all your problems would go away. See what a failure you are?"

"Yeah...that person you love so much? They aren't proud of you. You just aren't enough."

"You are such a bad person, no wonder you have lost friends."

"As soon as others realize what a disaster you are they will leave you too. And you will be all alone."

No wonder I am a warrior when I don't even think I am. Some days I feel like I am fighting a raging war all by myself. It makes me think of the movie series of *Star Wars.* [1] Over this last Christmas holiday we decided to watch the entire series. In one scene, I remember Obi Wan surrounded by circle of drone enemies. If you have never seen *Star Wars* you might not know exactly what drone enemies are but they all look the same and even use the same weapons to take you down. The enemies that wanted to destroy Obi Wan were not very creative in their ways to have taken him down. They were trained to fight, kill and destroy. However, Obi Wan had been trained differently. He had been trained as a Jedi to fight the enemy in creative ways. He didn't run from the fight. He faced it head on.

I found it interesting in the fourth movie when Princess Leia said, *"Help me Obi Wan Kenobi. You're my only hope."* Wow. Just think if he had lost his hope in those battles. The hope would not be able to be transferred to help another.

I believe that is what God wants us to understand. His Word is a powerful weapon to fight thoughts that all have the same agenda. The agenda to cause you to lose any hope and surrender in the battle. This is such a revelation that we are all warriors. Sometimes we may not believe that we are. We may even tell ourselves that is farther from the truth!

The reality is we are fighting. EVERY. SINGLE. DAY.

It may be fighting for things like:

- Hope
- Faith
- Forgiveness
- Love
- Courage
- Disability
- Depression
- Anger
- Resentfulness
- Loneliness
- Sickness
- Fatigue
- Self-Worth

The list can go on and on. It's what the enemy wants us to believe and will say to you, *"Why fight!? There is always something and you might as just well get used to it; give up now so you don't have to deal with all this pain of fighting."* Oh, that enemy. It is smart and cunning in the way it comes into our hearts to wound. It is designed to destroy, to kill off any and all that is of light that God wants you to access. It is just like those drones...

> *"Be alert and of sober mind. Your enemy the devil prowls around like*
> *a roaring lion looking for someone to devour."*
> I Peter 5:8

So how do we fight?

Ephesians 6 has been given us a blueprint of the battle to remind us that we can OVERCOME. With HIM by our side we can overcome and in fact the victory is already waiting for us to claim. It reminds me of a song that I heard when I was little.

> *We shall overcome, we shall triumph.*
> *We shall stand in the victory as one.*
> *Calvary's hill's been conquered by the Lord and King*
> *So, the victory is already won.*[2]

That is why I am a Warrior of Hope. I am also a warrior of faith, love, forgiveness and so much more for God has called me to be HIS warrior and to stand firm in his promise that when we keep our eyes on him and we put our trust in him that Hope will be everlasting.

I am a path-carver because I have hope in the healing God can give by my actions and work that He has called me to do. I have hope that when I finish here on this earth and meet Him someday that He will say, *"Well done my child, my Warrior. You have stood for me. You have fought the good fight and you are now being greatly rewarded."*

I know beyond a shadow of a doubt that the enemy wants us to suffocate any flame of hope that lies within us. He does not want your message to bless people. He doesn't want your story of love and transformation of God working through you to be heard. He will be relentless in trying to take it all from you using those closest to you to do His dirty work. This is why we must keep our eyes on him and guard against the forces that can rise up against you.

"I keep my eyes always on the Lord.
With him at my right hand, I will not be shaken."
Psalm 3:3

I want you to be a Warrior fighting for Hope. I want you to know how to fight, when to fight and why you must fight. As my pastor, Steven Furtick, has said, *"The greater the opposition, the greater the blessing."*

So, stand firm Warrior. Use this book and HIS word to strengthen your spirit. These stories took courage to share the message of Hope. That is why I knew the book *"Stepping Into Courage"* was to be before this book on Hope for in even the smallest steps of courage hope can be re-ignited like gasoline to a fire that looks like it's almost out.

I know this is why God gives me the spiritual gifts of prophesy and of communication because He has me holding the sword to stand for the Word of God and the worship that ignites the movement of the Holy Spirit. I share this because a little over two years ago I was given a song. I thought it was just my song for getting me through my hardship but now I realize that He works through and in me to deliver all my writings and my gifts of communication.

I keep my eyes on you
I keep my eyes on you
I put my trust in you
I put my trust in you

Oh God please help me stand
Oh please just hold my hand
Help me to light the way
I'll listen as I pray

I'll keep my eyes on you
I'll keep my eyes on you

I'll put my Hope in you
I'll put my Hope in you
I'll keep my Faith with you
I'll keep my Faith with you

Oh God please help me stand
Oh please just hold my hand
Help me to light the way
I'll listen as I pray

So, I'll have my hope in you
I'll have my hope in you

~ Lyrics and Melody by Tricia Andreassen

STRATEGIES FOR IGNITING YOUR FIRE OF HOPE:

1. What are some of the things the enemy has told you to cause your hope and your spirit to weaken?

_____

_____

_____

_____

2. Look for scriptures right now that help you battle the situation you are in and that will strengthen you.

For example: You are feeling like you never do anything right.

You put in an internet search and you find: Psalm 37:23-24 *"The LORD makes firm the steps of the one who delights in him; though he may stumble, he will not fall, for the LORD upholds him with his hand."*

_____

_____

_____

_____

_____

_____

_____

Note: I am making a commitment to create a devotional journal for you to write in called *Words for the Warrior* to help you combat these situations.

[1] Lucas, George, director Star Wars, Twentieth Century Fox
[2] Nelon Music Group

MY HOPE RISES

By Tricia Andreassen

MY HOPE RISES

I remember going to *Rising Hope Farms* for the first time. I felt like it was a dream come true as I drove on the gravel, curvy drive with woods on my right and large corn stalks on my left. Coming around the bed and seeing the red arena and the big barn behind it a feeling I couldn't explain flowed all over me.

The feeling was hope.

I didn't even know it at the time. For over a year I had been having dreams of horses but didn't understand it completely. I had been around horses all my childhood as when I was just in elementary school my friend had a farm and her horse *"Snooks"* rode us bare back and let us love all over him. That was my first experience of feeling the love from such a majestic creature.

In my middle school years my parent's friends owned a horse farm and their daughter taught me a lot about caring and brushing. One particular spring or summer their horse had a baby. Seeing the trust develop as I visited every weekend was something that I know now was special. Back then, as a child I didn't know how lucky I was to spend time with this little one. During that time of my life I don't have a lot of clear memories as that was an unhappy time in my childhood. I will save that for another time but what I will share is how often I would practically beg to go over and stay for the day. I didn't want to leave there. In West Virginia where we would go for the weekends, there was Pipestem State Park and I rode often there too. I remember I went so much the people in charge of the horses knew me by name. These horses over my childhood brought sparks of joy and connection.

So, when finding *Rising Hope Farm* by car and turning down that curvy gravel road you might imagine how my heart began to feel a rebirth of some kind. I didn't even realize it until a year later but I had visited Rising Hope on the web and had shared it on my Facebook page saying *"I see working here someday."* During that posting I didn't know where the farm was but I knew it was at least 30 minutes north of me. I share this because just 2 months after posting that on Facebook we found a home just a few miles from this place. It was a miracle. A miracle birthing hope.

Rising Hope Farms has become a special place for me. My favorite thing to do is to visit the horses early in the morning and do my devotional as well as writing there. One morning, Prophet, who is a horse who had been rescued from abuse years ago, was snuggling his nose into my chest. While holding each other I began to sing this song. I knew in the song where it says, *"Because of you,"* the YOU meant the Lord and the Horse. The song could be sung with my Heavenly Father one minute and to this glorious horse the next. I weaved all the names of the horses at *Rising Hope Farms* into my song so they knew they were loved and thanked for what they did for all the handicapped, mentally challenged and those overcoming trauma.

Because of you
My Hope Rises
Because of you
I can be strong
Because of you
I keep on going
Because of you
I feel restored

You brought me life
You've brought me joy
You've brought a miracle in my life
I'm thankful for all the blessings
You give to me
You give to me
Because of you
My Hope Rises
Because of you
I can be strong

Because of you
I keep on going
Because of you

I feel restored
You make me feel like warrior Gideon

Running through the darkest night
You see in me like a big Ole' Prophet
Shining Heaven down to me

Because of you
My Hope Rises
Because of you
I can be strong
Because of you
I keep on going
Because of you
I feel reborn

No one probably even knows still because I don't talk about it, but he and I had connected strongly with one another. I have cried quiet tears and have had pure joy with him. I can sincerely say that he has been a special horse in my life and the others have carved a special place in my heart too. To watch a disabled child be on the horse with his hands raised to heaven and experiencing complete freedom is something that I will never get tired of. Doing photography on the farm has been very special as I am able to capture the moments that can be remembered forever. Just like the written word, the legacy of *Rising Hope Farms* is a reminder of God's unfailing love. I get inspired when I see the volunteers give their time, patience and care into this ministry for the sake of bringing hope to all who come to this glorious place, www.RisingHopeFarms.org. This farm has inspired me to start a nonprofit called the Unstoppable Warrior Foundation to help those who have endured loss, trauma or abuse.

Rising Hope Farms and the people who give their time so freely reminds me that we can be a beacon of hope in many ways to others. That is what my heart yearns to do. I want to be that light for others too.

"Even so, let your light shine before men, that they may see your good works, and glorify your Father who is in Heaven."
Matthew 5:16

ABOUT TRICIA ANDREASSEN

Tricia Andreassen has a fire within her heart that started when she was a youth camp counselor. *"My mission is to bring teachings and life strategies to help break through struggles and obstacles that may arise. We all have a purpose and calling for our lives and I want as many people as possible to discover what their heart calls them to do."*

Tricia's unique combination of walking this path allows her to help others fulfill their life dreams. As an entrepreneur herself, Tricia bought her first real estate investment property at age 19. Her passion for growing leaders led her to be a National Speaker and Trainer for Realtor.com®, the official internet site of the National Association of REALTORS® (NAR). After seeing a deeper need to help real estate agents and teams develop their business plans, brands, websites and marketing messages, she started Pro Step Marketing from the bonus room of her house with her toddler son literally on her hip. She grew Pro Step Marketing into a leading marketing, web development, coaching and strategic planning company in the real estate niche; creating strategies and plans for more than 50% of the top REALTORS® listed in production for the Wall Street Journal. After almost 15 years as CEO, she sold her company.

In 2007 another life shift happened within Tricia's soul, and she began writing songs. Her heart yearned to help others through life challenges due to her own discoveries within herself. The unlocking of this spiritual and creative heartbeat in her opened her dreams of recording her own CD, singing at a national conference with over 7,000 in attendance and writing her first business book which has led to writing for magazines, news organizations, personal development and fiction. As her journey progresses, she evangelizes the message of persistence, resilience, faith and other life strategies with the spiritual gifts of soul healing work. Her passion is to deliver God's word and inspiration through writing books, speaking, teaching, singing and songwriting that speak resilience and life transformation.

Over the last 25+ years she has helped thousands of people in their lives and business. One of her companies, Creative Life Publishing and Learning Institute supports this mission of helping writers become authors as well as fostering teaching and training programs in faith, leadership, youth, parenting, business building, marketing and spiritual growth. All the authors that are published are personally interviewed and selected by Tricia with the highest integrity. Tricia's business and marketing book hit number one in less than five hours and was continually on the best-seller list for 59 weeks. She is also a Certified Speaker and Coach for the John Maxwell Organization to teach leadership, personal growth and youth development programs as well as a Certified Executive Coach through ACTP credentials for the International Coaching Federation, which enlists uniquely creative strategies to work with organizations, schools, ministry groups and leaders from all walks of life. In addition to this work she is an active speaker, songwriter and singer.

To inquire about Tricia speaking at your next event email Warrior@ MsUnstoppable.com or visit www.MsUnstoppable.com. If you have a story or message inside of you that could bring positive changes to others or a desire to be an author or speaker please reach out to Tricia today for a confidential conversation. To book Tricia as a speaker for your next event or to lead a retreat, a call with Tricia is essential as the first step to assure that she helps you achieve the outcome for success. Not all topics are listed on her website as some are designed custom for her clients and the specific topic of the event. She is also available for sermons and worship singing at your church or faith based conference.

Contact Tricia:

- Website: www.MsUnstoppable.com
- LinkedIn: www.LinkedIn.com/in/TriciaAndreassen
- Facebook: www.Facebook.com/UnstoppableWarrior
- YouTube: www.UnstoppableWarriorWithin.net
- Twitter: www.Twitter.com/TriciaSings
- Instagram: www.Instagram.com/MsUnstoppableWarrior
- Radio Show: www.UnlockYourInnerWarrior.com

Made in the USA
Lexington, KY
09 March 2018